*Aias*

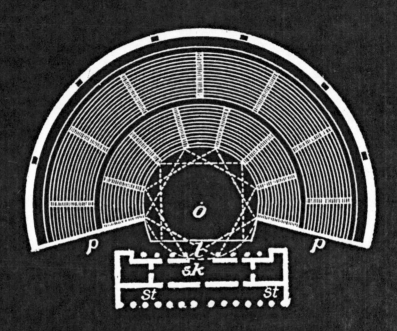

## ALSO BY JAMES SCULLY

*Modern Poetics*, ed. (McGraw-Hill) / *Modern Poets on Modern Poetry*, ed.
(Wm. Collins, Ltd.)

*The Marches* (Holt, Rinehart & Winston)

*Avenue of the Americas* (University of Massachusetts Press)

*Santiago Poems* (Curbstone Press)

*Aeschylus' Prometheus Bound*,
co-translated with C. John Herington (Oxford University Press)

*Quechua Peoples Poetry*,
co-translated with Maria A. Proser (Curbstone Press)

*Scrap Book* (Ziesling Brothers)

*De Repente / All of a Sudden* by Teresa de Jesùs,
co-translated with Maria A. Proser and Arlene Scully

*May Day* (Minnesota Review Press)

*Apollo Helmet* (Curbstone Press)

*Line Break: Poetry as Social Practice*
(Bay Press, Curbstone Press, Northwestern University Press)

*Raging Beauty: Selected Poems* (Azul Editions)

*Donatello's Version* (Curbstone Press)

*Oceania* (Azul Editions)

*Vagabond Flags* journal (Azul Editions)

*Angel in Flames: Selected Poems & Translations*
(Smokestack Books, UK)

*The Complete Plays of Sophocles* with Robert Bagg
(Harper Perennial)

# AIAS

*A New Translation by James Scully*

## SOPHOCLES

HARPER PERENNIAL

NEW YORK • LONDON • TORONTO • SYDNEY • NEW DELHI • AUCKLAND

HARPER PERENNIAL

For performance rights to *Aias* contact The Strothman Agency, LLC, at 197 Eighth Street, Flagship Wharf – 611, Charlestown, MA 02129, or by email at info@strothmanagency.com.

FIRST EDITION

*Designed by Justin Dodd*

Library of Congress Cataloging-in-Publication Data is available upon request.

ISBN 978-0-06-213214-7

12 13 14 15 16 /RRD   10 9 8 7 6 5 4 3 2 1

*For the many teachers and interpreters who have held to,
and communicated, the living historicity of these plays*

# CONTENTS

# WHEN THEATER WAS LIFE: THE WORLD OF SOPHOCLES

I

Greek theater emerged from the same explosive creativity that propelled the institutions and ways of knowing of ancient Athens, through two and a half millennia, into our own era. These ranged from the concept and practice of democracy, to an aggressive use of logic with few holds barred, to a philosophy singing not of gods and heroes but of what exists, where it came from, and why. Athenians distinguished history from myth, acutely observed the human form, and reconceived medicine from a set of beliefs and untheorized practices into a science.

Playwrights, whose work was presented to audiences of thousands, effectively took center stage as critics and interpreters of their own culture. Athenian drama had one major showing each year at the nine-day Festival of Dionysos. It was rigorously vetted. Eight dramatists (three tragedians, five comic playwrights), chosen in open competition, were "granted choruses," a down-to-earth term meaning that the city financed production of their plays. For the Athenians theater was as central to civic life as the assembly, law courts, temples, and agora.

Historians summing up Athens' cultural importance have tended to emphasize its glories, attending less to the brutal institutions and policies that underwrote the city's wealth and dominance: its slaves, for instance, who worked the mines that enriched the communal treasury; or its policy of executing the men and enslaving the women and children of enemy cities that refused to surrender on demand. During its long war with Sparta, Athens' raw and unbridled democracy became increasingly reckless, cruel, and eventually self-defeating. Outside the assembly's daily debates on war, peace, and myriad other issues, Athenian citizens, most notably the indefatigable Socrates, waged ongoing critiques of the city's actions and principles. Playwrights, whom the Athenians called *didaskaloi* (educators), were expected to enlighten audiences about themselves, both individually and collectively. As evidenced by the thirty-three plays that survive, these works presented a huge audience annually with conflicts and dilemmas of the most extreme sort.

To some extent all Sophocles' plays engage personal, social, and political crises and confrontations—not just those preserved in heroic legend but those taking place in his immediate world. Other Athenian intellectuals, including Thucydides, Aeschylus, Euripides, Plato, and Aristophanes, were part of that open-ended discussion in which everything was subject to question, including the viability of the city and its democracy (which was twice voted temporarily out of existence).

## II

To this day virtually every Athenian theatrical innovation—from paraphernalia such as scenery, costumes, and masks to the architecture of stage and seating and, not least, to the use of drama as a powerful means of cultural and political commentary—remains in use. We thus inherit from Athens the vital *potential* for drama to engage our realities and to support or critique prevailing orthodoxies.

The myths that engaged Sophocles' audience originated in Homer's epics of the Trojan War and its aftermath. Yet Homer's world was tribal. That of the Greek tragedians was not, or only nominally so. With few exceptions (e.g., Aeschylus' *The Persians*), those playwrights were writing *through* the Homeric world to address, and deal with, the *polis* world they themselves were living in. Sophocles was appropriating stories and situations from these epics, which were central to the mythos of Athenian culture, and re-visioning them into dramatic *agons* (contests) relevant to the tumultuous, often vicious politics of Greek life in the fifth century BCE. Today some of Sophocles' concerns, and the way he approached them, correspond at their deepest levels to events and patterns of thought and conduct that trouble our own time. For example, "[Sophocles'] was an age when war was endemic. And Athens in the late fifth century BC appeared to have a heightened taste for conflict. One year of two in the Democratic Assembly, Athenian citizens voted in favor of military aggression" (Hughes, 138).

Each generation interprets and translates these plays in keeping with the style and idiom it believes best suited for tragedy.

Inevitably even the most skilled at preserving the original's essentials, while attuning its voice to the present, will eventually seem the relic of a bygone age. We have assumed that a contemporary translation should attempt to convey not only what the original seems to have been communicating, but *how* it communicated—not in its saying, only, but in its *doing*. It cannot be said too often: these plays were social and historical *events* witnessed by thousands in a context and setting infused with religious ritual and civic protocol. They were not transitory, one-off entertainments but were preserved, memorized, and invoked. Respecting this basic circumstance will not guarantee a successful translation, but it is a precondition for giving these works breathing room in which their strangeness, their rootedness in distinct historical moments, can flourish. As with life itself, they were not made of words alone.

Athenian playwrights relied on a settled progression of scene types: usually a prologue followed by conversations or exchanges in which situations and attitudes are introduced, then a series of confrontations that feature cut-and-thrust dialogue interrupted by messenger narratives, communal songs of exultation or grieving, and less emotionally saturated, or 'objective,' choral odes that respond to or glance off the action. Audiences expected chorus members to be capable of conveying the extraordinary range of expressive modes, from the pithy to the operatic, that Sophocles had at his disposal. To translate this we have needed the resources not only of idiomatic English but also of rhetorical gravitas and, on occasion, colloquial English. Which is why we have adopted, regarding vocabulary and 'levels of speech,' a wide and varied palette. When Philoktetes

exclaims, "You said it, boy," that saying corresponds in character to the colloquial Greek expression. On the other hand Aias's
"Long rolling waves of time . . ." is as elevated, without being
pompous, as anything can be.

Unfortunately we've been taught, and have learned to live
with, washed-out stereotypes of the life and art of 'classical'
times—just as we have come to associate Greek sculpture with
the color of its underlying material, usually white marble. The
classical historian Bettany Hughes writes in *The Hemlock Cup*
(81) that temples and monuments were painted or stained in
"Technicolor" to be seen under the bright Attic sun. The stat-
ues' eyes were not blanks gazing off into space. They had color:
a *look*. To restore their flesh tones, their eye color, and the
bright hues of their cloaks would seem a desecration. We should
understand that this is so—even as we recognize that, for us,
there is no going back. We've been conditioned to preserve not
the reality of ancient Greek sculpture in its robust cultural am-
bience and physical setting, but our own fixed conception of it
as colorless and sedate—a perception created, ironically, by the
weathering and ravages of centuries. No one can change that.
Still, as translators we have a responsibility not to reissue a ste-
reotype of classical Greek culture but rather to recoup, to the
extent possible, the vitality of its once living reality.

Regarding its highly inflected language, so different from our
more context-driven modern English, we recognize that locu-
tions sounding contorted, coy, recondite, or annoyingly round-
about were a feature of ordinary Greek and were intensified in
theatrical discourse. Highly wrought, larger-than-life expressions, delivered without artificial amplification to an audience

of thousands, did not jar when resonating in the vast Theater of Dionysos, but may to our own Anglophone ears when delivered from our more intimate stages and screens, or read in our books and electronic tablets. Accordingly, where appropriate, and especially in rapid exchanges, we have our characters speak more straightforwardly—as happens in Greek stichomythia, when characters argue back and forth in alternating lines (or 'rows') of verse, usually linked by a word they hold in common. Here, for example, is a snippet from *Aias* (1305–1309) that pivots on "right," "killer," "dead" and "god(s)":

TEUKROS    A righteous cause is my courage.
MENELAOS   What? It's right to defend my killer?
TEUKROS    Your killer!? You're dead? And still alive?
MENELAOS   A god saved me. But he *wanted* me dead.
TEUKROS    If the gods saved you, why disrespect them?

There are no rules for determining when a more-literal or less-literal approach is appropriate. Historical and dramatic context have to be taken into account. The objective is not only to render the textual meaning (which is ordinarily more on the phrase-by-phrase than the word-by-word level) but also to communicate the feel and impact embedded in that meaning. Dictionaries are indispensable for translators, but they are not sufficient. The meanings of words are immeasurably more nuanced and wide-ranging in life than they can ever be in a lexicon. As in life, where most 'sayings' cannot be fully grasped apart from their timing and their place in both personal and social contexts, so in theater: dramatic context must take words up and finish them off. In *Aias*, Teukros, the out-of-wedlock half brother of Aias, and Menelaos, co-commander of the Greek forces, are trading insults. When Menelaos says, "The archer, far from blood dust, thinks he's something," Teukros quietly rejoins, "I'm very good at what I do" (1300–1301).

Understanding the exchange between the two men requires that the reader or audience recognize the 'class' implications of archery. Socially and militarily, archers rank low in the pecking order. They stand to the rear of the battle formation. Archers are archers usually because they can't afford the armor one needs to be a hoplite, a frontline fighter. The point is that Teukros refuses to accept 'his place' in the social and military order. For a Greek audience, the sheer fact of standing his ground against a commander had to have been audacious. But that is not how it automatically registers in most modern word-by-word translations, which tend to make Teukros sound defensive (a trait wholly out of his character in this play). Examples: (a) "Even so, 'tis no sordid craft that I possess," (b) "I'm not the master of a menial skill," (c) "My archery is no contemptible science," (d) "The art I practice is no mean one." These translations are technically accurate. They're scrupulous in reproducing the Greek construction whereby, in an idiomatic context, a negative may register as an assertion—or even, framed as a negative future question, become a command. But tonally, in modern English idiom, Teukros' negation undercuts his assertion (the 'I'm not . . . but even so' formula). To our ears it admits weakness or defensiveness. "I'm very good at what I do," however, is a barely veiled threat. The dramatic arc of the encounter, which confirms that Teukros will not back down for anything or anyone, not even a commander of the Greek army, substantiates that Sophocles meant it to be heard as such.

Hearing the line in context we realize instantly not only what the words are saying but, more pointedly and feelingly, what they're doing. His words are not just 'about' something. They are an act in themselves—not, as in the more literal translations, a duress-driven apologia. Translation must thus respond to an individual character's ever-changing demeanor and circumstance. The speaker's state of mind should show through his or her words, just as in life. Idiomatic or colloquial expressions fit many situations better—especially those that have a more finely tuned emotional economy—–than phrases that, if uninhabited, hollowed out, or just plain buttoned-up, sound evasive or euphemistic. Many of the speeches Sophocles gives his characters are as abrupt and common as he might himself have spoken to his fellow Athenians in the assembly, in the agora, to his troops, his actors, or his family.

At times we have chosen a more literal translation in passages where scholars have opted for a seemingly more accessible modern phrase. At the climactic moment in *Oedipus the King*, when Oedipus realizes he has killed his father and fathered children with his mother, he says in a modern prose version by Hugh Lloyd-Jones: "Oh, oh! All is now clear. O light, may I now look on you for the last time, I who am revealed as cursed in my birth, cursed in my marriage, cursed in my killing!" (Greek 1182–1885). When Lloyd-Jones uses and repeats the word "cursed," he is compressing a longer Greek phrase meaning "being shown to have done what must not be done." This compression shifts the emphasis from his unsuspecting human actions toward the realm of the god who acted to "curse" him. The following lines keep the original grammatical construction:

> All! All! It has all happened!
> It was all true. O light! Let this
> be the last time I look on you.
> You see now who I am—
> the child who must not be born!
> I loved where I must not love!
> I killed where I must not kill! (1336–1342)

Here Oedipus names the three acts of interfamilial transgression that it was both his good and his ill fortune to have survived, participated in, and inflicted—birth, sexual love, and murder in self-defense—focusing not only on the curse each act has become but now realizing the full and horrific consequence of each action that was, as it happened, unknowable. Registering the shudder rushing through him, Oedipus's exclamations convey the shock of his realization: *I did these things without feeling their horror as I do now.*

Finally, translations tend to be more or less effective depending on their ability to convey the emotional and physiological reactions that will give a reader or an audience a kinesthetic relationship to the dramatic moment, whether realized as text or performance. This is a precondition for maintaining the tactility that characterizes any living language. Dante wrote that the spirit of poetry abounds "in the tangled constructions and defective pronunciations" of vernacular speech where language is renewed and transformed. We have not attempted that—these are translations, not new works—but we have striven for a language that is spontaneous and generative as opposed to one that is studied and bodiless. We have also worked to preserve the root meaning of Sophocles' Greek, especially his always illuminating metaphors.

## III

Sophocles reveals several recurrent attitudes in his plays—sympathy for fate's victims, hostility toward leaders who abuse their power, skepticism toward self-indulgent 'heroes,' disillusionment with war and revenge—that are both personal and politically significant. All his plays to a greater or lesser degree focus on outcasts from their communities. Historically, those who transgress a community's values have either been physically exiled or stigmatized by sanctions and/or shunning. To keep a polity from breaking apart, everyone, regardless of social standing, must abide by certain enforceable communal expectations. Athens in the fifth century BCE practiced political ostracism, a procedure incorporated in its laws. By voting to ostracize a citizen, Athens withdrew its protection and civic benefits—sometimes to punish an offender, but also as a kind of referee's move, expelling a divisive public figure from the city (and from his antagonists) so as to promote a ten-year period of relative peace.

In earlier eras Greek cities also cast out those who committed sacrilege. Murderers of kin, for instance, or blasphemers of a god—in myth and in real life—were banished from Greek cities until the 'unclean' individual 'purged' his crime according to current religious custom. The imperative to banish a kin violator runs so deep that Oedipus, after discovering he has committed patricide and incest, passes judgment on himself and demands to live in exile. In *Oedipus at Kolonos*, he and Antigone have been exiled from Thebes against their will. In the non-Oedipus plays the title characters Philoktetes, Elektra, and Aias, as well as Herakles in *Women of Trakhis*, are not outcasts in the traditional sense, though all have actively or involuntarily offended their social units in some way. They may or may not be typical tragic characters; nonetheless none 'fit' the world they're given to live in. In these translations we've incorporated awareness of social dimensions in the original texts, which, as they involve exercises of power, are no less political than social.

In each of the four non-Oedipus plays, a lethal confrontation or conflict 'crazes' the surface coherence of a society (presumed to be Athenian society, either in itself or as mediated through a military context), thus revealing and heightening its internal contradictions.

In *Women of Trakhis* the revered hero Herakles, when he tries to impose a young concubine on his wife Deianeira, provokes her to desperate measures that unwittingly cause him horrific pain, whereupon he exposes his savage and egomaniacal nature, lashing out at everyone around him, exercising a hero's prerogatives so savagely that he darkens his own reputation and drives his wife to suicide and his son to bitter resentment.

*Elektra* exposes the dehumanizing cost of taking revenge, by revealing the neurotic, materialistic, and cold-blooded character of the avengers. In *Aias*, when the Greek Army's most powerful soldier tries to assassinate his commanders, whose authority rests on dubious grounds, he exposes not only them but his own growing obsolescence in a prolonged war that has more need of strategic acumen, as exemplified by Odysseus, than brute force. In *Philoktetes* the title character, abandoned on a deserted island because of a stinking wound his fellow warriors can't live with, is recalled to active service with the promise of a cure and rehabilitation. The army needs him and his bow to win the war. It is a call he resists, until the god Herakles negotiates a resolution—not in the name of justice, but because Philoktetes' compliance is culturally mandated. As in *Aias*, the object is to maintain the integrity and thus the survival of the society itself. The greatest threat is not an individual's death, which here is not the preeminent concern, but the disintegration of a society.

In our own time aspects of *Aias* and *Philoktetes* have been used for purposes that Sophocles, who was the sponsor in Athens of a healing cult, might have appreciated. Both heroes, but especially Aias, have been appropriated as exemplars of posttraumatic stress disorder, in particular as suffered by soldiers in and out of a war zone. Excerpts from these two plays have been performed around the United States for veterans, soldiers on active duty, their families, and concerned others. Ultimately, however, Sophocles is intent on engaging and resolving internal contradictions that threaten the historical continuity, the very future, of the Athenian city-state. He invokes the class contradictions Athens was experiencing by applying them to the mythical/historical eras from which he draws his plots.

Modern-day relevancies implicit in Sophocles' plays will come sharply into focus or recede from view depending on time and circumstance. The constant factors in these plays will always be their consummate poetry, dramatic propulsion, and the intensity with which they illuminate human motivation and morality. Scholars have also identified allusions in his plays to events in Athenian history. The plague in *Oedipus the King* is described in detail so vivid it dovetails in many respects with Thucydides' more clinical account of the plague that killed one-third to one-half of Athens' population beginning in 429 BCE. Kreon, Antigone's antagonist, displays the imperviousness to rational advice and lack of foresight exhibited by the politicians of Sophocles' era, whose follies Thucydides narrates, and which Sophocles himself was called in to help repair—specifically by taking a democracy that in a fit of imperial overreach suffered, in 413, a catastrophic defeat on the shores of Sicily, and replacing it with a revanchist oligarchy. When Pisander, one of the newly empowered oligarchs, asked Sophocles if he was one of the councilors who had approved the replacement of the democratic assembly by what was, in effect, a junta of four hundred, Sophocles admitted that he had. "Why?" asked Pisander. "Did you not think this a terrible decision?" Sophocles agreed it was. "So weren't you doing something terrible?" "That's right. There was no better alternative." (Aristotle, Rh. 1419a). The lesson? When life, more brutally than drama, delivers its irreversible calamities and judgments, it forces a polity, most movingly, to an utterly unanticipated, wholly 'other' moral and spiritual level.

In *Oedipus at Kolonos* Sophocles alludes to his city's decline when he celebrates a self-confident Athens that no longer existed when Sophocles wrote that play. He gives us Theseus, a throwback to the type of thoughtful, decisive, all-around leader Athens lacked as it pursued policies that left it impoverished and defenseless—this under the delusion that its only enemies were Spartans and Sparta's allies.


## IV

Archaeologists have identified scores of local theaters all over the Greek world—stone semicircles, some in cities and at religious destinations, others in rural villages. Within many of these structures both ancient and modern plays are still staged. Hillsides whose slopes were wide and gentle enough to seat a crowd made perfect settings for dramatic encounters and were the earliest theaters. Ancient roads that widened below a gentle hillside, or level ground at a hill's base, provided suitable performance spaces. Such sites, along with every city's agora and a temple dedicated to Dionysos or another god, were the main arenas of community activity. Stone tablets along roads leading to theaters commemorated local victors: athletes, actors, playwrights, singers, and the winning plays' producers. Theaters, in every sense, were open to all the crosscurrents of civic and domestic life.

The components of the earliest theaters reflect their rural origins and were later incorporated into urban settings. *Theatron*, the root of our word "theater," translates as "viewing place" and designated the curved and banked seating area. *Orchestra* was literally "the place for dancing." The costumed actors emerged from and retired to the *skenê*, a word that originally meant, and literally was in the rural theaters, a tent. As theaters evolved to become more permanent structures, the *skenê* developed as well into a "stage building" whose painted facade changed, like a mask, with the characters' various habitats. Depending on the drama, the *skenê* could assume the appearance of a king's grand palace, the Kyklops' cave, a temple to a god, or (reverting to its original material form) an army commander's tent.

Greek drama itself originated in two earlier traditions, one rural, one civic. Choral singing of hymns to honor Dionysos or other gods and heroes, which had begun in the countryside, evolved into the structured choral ode. The costumes and the dancing of choral singers, often accompanied by a reed instrument, are depicted on sixth-century vases that predate the plays staged in the Athenian theater. The highly confrontational nature of every play suggests how early choral odes and dialogues came into being in concert with a fundamental aspect of democratic governance: public and spirited debate. Two or more characters facing off in front of an audience was a situation at the heart of both drama and democratic politics.

Debate, the democratic Athenian art practiced and perfected by politicians, litigators, and thespians—relished and judged by voters, juries, and audiences—flourished in theatrical venues and permeated daily Athenian life. Thucydides used it to narrate his history of the war between Athens and Sparta. He recalled scores of lengthy debates that laid out the motives of politicians, generals, and diplomats as each argued his case for a particular policy or a strategy. Plato, recognizing the open-ended, exploratory power of spirited dialogue, wrote his philosophy entirely in dramatic form.

The Greeks were addicted to contests and turned virtually every chance for determining a winner into a formal competition. The Great Dionysia for playwrights and choral singers and the Olympics for athletes are only the most famous and familiar. The verbal *agon* remains to this day a powerful medium for testing and judging issues. And character, as in the debate between Teukros and Menelaos, may be laid bare. But there is no guarantee. Persuasiveness can be, and frequently is, manipulative (e.g., many of the sophists evolved into hired rhetorical guns, as distinguished from the truth-seeking, pre-Socratic philosophers). Sophocles may well have had the sophists' amorality in mind when he had Odysseus persuade Neoptomolos that betraying Philoktetes would be a patriotic act and bring the young man fame.

Though they were part of a high-stakes competition, the plays performed at the Dionysia were part of a religious ceremony whose chief purpose was to honor theater's patron god, Dionysos. The god's worshippers believed that Dionysos' powers and rituals transformed the ways in which they experienced and dealt with their world—from their enthralled response to theatrical illusion and disguise to the exhilaration, liberation, and violence induced by wine. Yet the festival also aired, or licensed, civic issues that might otherwise have had no truly public, *polis*-wide expression. The playwrights wrote as *politai*, civic poets, as distinguished from those who focused on personal lyrics and shorter choral works. Though *Aias* and *Philoktetes* are set in a military milieu, the issues they engage are essentially civil and political. Neither *Aias* nor *Philoktetes* is concerned with the 'enemy of record,' Troy, but rather with Greek-on-Greek conflict. With civil disruption, and worse. In fact one need look no further than the play venue itself for confirmation of the interpenetration of the civic with the military—a concern bordering on preoccupation—when, every year, the orphans of warriors killed in battle were given new hoplite armor and a place of honor at the Festival of Dionysos.

Communal cohesiveness and the historical continuity of the polity are most tellingly threatened from within: in *Aias* by the individualistic imbalance and arrogance of Aias, whose warrior qualities and strengths are also his weakness—they lead him to destroy the war spoil that is the common property of the entire Greek army—and in *Philoktetes* by the understandable and just, yet inordinately unyielding, self-preoccupation of Philoktetes himself. In both cases the fundamental, encompassing question is this: With what understandings, what basic values, is the commonality of the *polis* to be recovered and rededicated in an era in which civic cohesiveness is under the extreme pressure of a war Athens is losing (especially at the time *Philoktetes* was produced) and, further, the simmering stasis of unresolved class or caste interests? In sharply different ways, all three plays of the Oedipus cycle, as well as *Aias* and *Elektra*, cast doubt on the legitimacy of usurped, authoritarian, or publicly disapproved leadership.

Given the historical and political dynamism of these great, instructive works, we've aimed to translate and communicate their challenge to Athenian values for a contemporary audience whose own values are no less under duress.

## V

The Great Dionysia was the central and most widely attended event of the political year, scheduled after winter storms had abated so that foreign visitors could come and bear witness to Athens' wealth, civic pride, imperial power, and artistic imagination. For eight or nine days each spring, during the heyday of Greek theater in the fifth century BCE, Athenians flocked to the temple grounds sacred to Dionysos on the southern slope of the Acropolis. After dark on the first day, a parade of young men hefted a giant phallic icon of the god from the temple and into the nearby theater. As the icon had been festooned with garlands of ivy and a mask of the god's leering face, their raucous procession initiated a dramatic festival called the City Dionysia, a name that differentiated it from the festival's ancient rural origins in Dionysian myth and cult celebrations of the god. As the festival gained importance in the sixth century BCE, most likely through the policies of Pisistratus, it was also known as the Great Dionysia.

Pisistratus, an Athenian tyrant in power off and on beginning in 561 BCE and continuously from 546 to 527, had good reason for adapting the Rural Dionysia as Athens' Great Dionysia: "Dionysos was a god for the 'whole' of democratic Athens" (Hughes, 213). Everyone, regardless of political faction or social standing, could relate to the boisterous communal activities of the festival honoring Dionysos: feasting, wine drinking, dancing, singing, romping through the countryside, and performing or witnessing dithyrambs and more elaborate dramatic works. The Great Dionysia thus served to keep in check, if not transcend, internal factionalizing by giving all citizens a 'natural' stake in Athens—Athens not simply as a place but as a venerable polity with ancient cultural roots. To this end Pisistratus had imported from Eleutherai an ancient phallic representation of Dionysos, one that took several men to carry.

Lodged as it was in a temple on the outskirts of Athens, this bigger-than-life icon gave the relatively new, citified cult the sanctified air of hoary antiquity (Csapo and Slater, 103–104). Thus validated culturally, the Great Dionysia was secured as a host to reassert, and annually rededicate, Athens as a democratic polity. As Bettany Hughes notes in *The Hemlock Cup*, "to call Greek drama an 'art-form' is somewhat anachronistic. The Greeks (unlike many modern-day bureaucrats) didn't distinguish drama as 'art'—something separate from 'society,' 'politics,' [or] 'life.' Theater was fundamental to democratic Athenian business. . . . [In] the fifth century this was the place where Athenian democrats came to understand the very world they lived in" (Hughes, 213).

The occasion offered Athens the chance to display treasure exacted from subjugated 'allies' (or tributes others willingly brought to the stage) and to award gold crowns to citizens whose achievements Athens' leaders wished to honor. Theater attendance itself was closely linked to citizenship; local town councils issued free festival passes to citizens in good standing. The ten generals elected yearly to conduct Athens' military campaigns poured libations to Dionysos. The theater's bowl seethed with a heady, sometimes unruly brew of military, political, and religious energy.

Performances began at dawn and lasted well into the

afternoon. The 14,000 or more Athenians present watched in god knows what state of anticipation or anxiety. Whatever else it did to entertain, move, and awe, Athenian tragedy consistently exposed human vulnerability to the gods' malice and favoritism. Because the gods were potent realities to Athenian audiences, they craved and expected an overwhelming emotional, physically distressing experience. That expectation distinguishes the greater intensity with which Athenians responded to plays from our own less challenging, more routine and frequent encounters with drama. Athenians wept while watching deities punish the innocent or unlucky, a reaction that distressed Plato. In his *Republic*, rather than question the motives or morality of the all-powerful Olympian gods for causing mortals grief, he blamed the poets and playwrights for their unwarranted wringing of the audience's emotions. He held that the gods had no responsibility for human suffering. True to form, Plato banned both poets and playwrights from his ideal city.

Modern audiences would be thoroughly at home with other, more cinematic stage effects. The sights and sounds tragedy delivered in the Theater of Dionysos were often spectacular. Aristotle, who witnessed a lifetime of productions in the fourth century—well after Sophocles' own lifetime, when the plays were performed in the heat of their historical moment—identified "spectacle," or *opsis*, as one of the basic (though to him suspect) elements of tragic theater. Under the influence of Aristotle, who preferred the study to the stage, and who therefore emphasized the poetry rather than the production of works, ancient commentators tended to consider "the visual aspects of drama [as] both vulgar and archaic" (Csapo and Slater, 257).

Nonetheless, visual and aural aspects there were: oboe music; dancing and the singing of set-piece odes by a chorus; masks that transformed the same male actor, for instance, into a swarthy-faced young hero, a dignified matron, Argos with a hundred eyes, or the Kyklops with only one. The theater featured painted scenery and large-scale constructions engineered with sliding platforms and towering cranes. It's hardly surprising that Greek tragedy has been considered a forerunner of Italian opera.

Judges awarding prizes at the Great Dionysia were chosen by lot from a list supplied by the council—one judge from each of Athens' ten tribes. Critical acumen was not required to get one's name on the list, but the *choregoi* (the producers and fi-nancial sponsors of the plays) were present when the jury was assembled and probably had a hand in its selection. At the con-clusion of the festival the ten selected judges, each having sworn that he hadn't been bribed or unduly influenced, would inscribe on a tablet the names of the three competing playwrights in descending order of merit. The rest of the process depended on chance. The ten judges placed their ballots in a large urn. The presiding official drew five at random, counted up the weighted vote totals, and declared the winner.

## VI

When Sophocles was a boy, masters trained him to excel in music, dance, and wrestling. He won crowns competing against his age-mates in all three disciplines. Tradition has it that he first appeared in Athenian national life at age fifteen, dancing naked (according to one source) and leading other boy dancers in a hymn of gratitude to celebrate Athens' defeat of the Persian fleet in the straits of Salamis.

Sophocles' father, Sophroniscus, manufactured weapons and armor (probably in a factory operated by slaves), and his mother, Phaenarete, was a midwife. The family lived in Kolonos, a rural suburb just north of Athens. Although his parents were not aristocrats, as most other playwrights' were, they surely had money and owned property; thus their status did not hamper their son's career prospects. Sophocles' talents as a dramatist, so formidable and so precociously developed, won him early fame. As an actor he triumphed in his own now-lost play, *Nausicaä*, in the role of the eponymous young princess who discovers the nearly naked Odysseus washed up on the beach while playing ball with her girlfriends.

During Sophocles' sixty-five-year career as a *didaskalos* he wrote and directed more than 120 plays and was awarded first prize at least eighteen times. No record exists of his placing lower than second. Of the seven entire works of his that survive, along with a substantial fragment of a satyr play, *The Trackers*, only two very late plays can be given exact production dates: *Philoktetes* in 409 and *Oedipus at Kolonos*, staged posthumously in 401. Some evidence suggests that *Antigone* was produced around 442–441 and *Oedipus the King* in the 420s. *Aias*, *Elektra*, and *Women of Trakhis* have been conjecturally, but never conclusively, dated through stylistic analysis. Aristotle, who had access we forever lack to the hundreds of fifth-century plays produced at the Dionysia, preferred Sophocles to his rivals Aeschylus and Euripides. He considered *Oedipus the King* the perfect example of tragic form, and developed his theory of tragedy from his analysis of it.

Sophocles' fellow citizens respected him sufficiently to vote him into high city office on at least three occasions. He served for a year as chief tribute-collector for Athens' overseas empire. A controversial claim by Aristophanes of Byzantium, in the third century, implies that Sophocles' tribe was so impressed by a production of *Antigone* that they voted him in as one of ten military generals (*strategoi*) in 441–440. Later in life Sophocles was respected as a participant in democratic governance at the highest level. In 411 he was elected to a ten-man commission charged with replacing Athens' discredited democratic governance with an oligarchy, a development that followed the military's catastrophic defeat in Sicily in 413.

Most ancient biographical sources attest to Sophocles' good looks, his easygoing manner, and his enjoyment of life. Athanaeus' multivolume *Deipnosophistai*, a compendium of gossip and dinner chat about and among ancient worthies, includes several vivid passages that reveal Sophocles as both a commanding presence and an impish prankster, ready one moment to put down a schoolmaster's boorish literary criticism and the next to flirt with the wine boy.

Sophocles is also convincingly described as universally respected, with amorous inclinations and intensely religious qualities that, to his contemporaries, did not seem incompatible. Religious piety meant something quite different to an Athenian than the humility, sobriety, and aversion to sensual pleasure it might suggest to us—officially, if not actually. His involvement in various cults, including one dedicated to a god of health and another to the hero Herakles, contributed to his reputation as "loved by the gods" and "the most religious of men." He was celebrated—and worshipped after his death as a hero—for bringing a healing cult (related to Aesculapius and involving a snake) to Athens. It is possible he founded an early version of a hospital. He never flinched from portraying the Greek gods as often wantonly cruel, destroying innocent people, for instance, as punishment for their ancestors' crimes. But the gods in *Antigone*, *Oedipus at Kolonos*, and *Philoktetes* mete out justice with a more even hand.

One remarkable absence in Sophocles' own life was documented suffering of any kind. His luck continued to the moment his body was placed in its tomb. As he lay dying, a Spartan army had once again invaded the Athenian countryside, blocking access to Sophocles' burial site beyond Athens' walls. But after Sophocles' peaceful death the Spartan general allowed the poet's burial party to pass through his lines, apparently out of respect for the god Dionysos.

Robert Bagg
James Scully

## NOTE

1. Unless otherwise indicated, the line numbers and note numbers for translations of Sophocles' dramas other than *Aias* refer to those in the Harper Perennial *Complete Sophocles* series.

*Aias*

# ACHILLES IS DEAD

A chilles is dead. Aias, the next greatest warrior, should inherit his armor, but Agamemnon and Menelaos award it to Odysseus. Enraged, Aias sets out to kill them, but Athena deludes him into slaughtering the war spoil of the Greek army: defenseless sheep, goats, oxen, and herdsmen. When Aias realizes what he has done, his shame is irremediable. He does then what no Greek hero ever does. He kills himself.

Heroic Aias epitomizes the aristocratic ethos of the Homeric world. Sophocles' play, however, was conceived four hundred to five hundred years after Homer's time, in the challenged democratic ethos of fifth-century BCE Athens. To Athenians, Aias's life was legendary. Roughly 10 percent of the population revered him as an ancestor. Homer shows him saving the Greek forces many times over. Accordingly—an occupational hazard of Greek warriors—he's full of himself. His lack of *sôphrosunê*, the wisdom to understand and accept his own limits and those of life itself, looms huge. When realization does come, it's too late. The "savage discipline" he learned as a warrior is so ingrained it has become his nature. He cannot choose to act outside it. He may regain his honor only by killing himself. Yet when he does do that—though he had seemed to be the center of the world, the focus of everyone's consciousness, their hopes and fears—the world doesn't end. Against all expectations, the play goes on over his lifeless body, which must be dealt with.

Aias's family and his sailor warriors are regrouping, preparing the body for burial. First Menelaos and then Agamemnon intervene, both insisting the remains be left as carrion for scavengers. Teukros argues with each in turn—until Odysseus arrives and pressures Agamemnon into letting the burial proceed. The obvious question is, why was it necessary to dwell, at such extraordinary length, on the conditions of Aias's burial?

Let's go back a bit. Between Aias's death and the discovery of his body, the Chorus, divided into two search parties, stumble about, disoriented, calling out to one another. Within this 'hole in time' (literally, a historical void), the play undergoes a definitive shift in historical and ideological perspective.[1] This is confirmed by Teukros, Aias's half brother, a lesser but not insignificant version of Aias himself. His exchanges with Menelaos and Agamemnon bring the tone and concerns of the play down, ingloriously, to an earth less cosmically resonant than the one we'd started out with. On these grounds, the terms of perception become those of fifth-century Athens. The heroic era has undone itself. We have witnessed its tragic end. Why then hasn't Sophocles left it at that?

Sophocles was considered not only a great playwright, but a great teacher.[2] The philosophically and theatrically difficult heart of *Aias* is his brilliant attempt to delimit and resolve a civic and historical conundrum: how does a political system, indeed a culture, adapt to new circumstances without self-destructing? Specifically, how does it make the transition from a monarchical/aristocratic tribal structure, in which the lives of all depend on heroic, bigger-than-life individuals, into an electoral republic sustained by the *inter*-dependence of all—who are not mythic but life-sized, yet who still bear the strains of ancient heroic values? How may this intensely but incompletely democratized culture honor the individualistic heroic legacy that never ceases informing it?[3] There are no final answers, nor is this the only way to frame the issues. Nonetheless, it is concerns of this order that drive the plot of *Aias*.

Aias is caught in the wrong kind of war. Objective conditions have changed; he cannot. Everyone has depended on him for their survival: family, his retinue of Salaminian marines, the Greek forces and their commanders. All have needed him to be a tower of strength—his brutishness not a flaw but, rather, crucial to his heroic stature. He has held the battle line when no one else could. Yet circumstances have rendered his *aretê* (his particular valor) obsolete. The war has become a quagmire. Now it's not the broad-shouldered who are needed, but those with brains—as the blunt-spoken Agamemnon puts it, comparing Aias to a big ox kept on the road by a little whip. The resourceful Odysseus (whose ingenuity ultimately conceived the Trojan horse) is the hero the Greeks really need.

During the original performance—presumably after Aias's death, as the language and social perspective of the play dropped down into an antiheroic, demythifying mode—the audience reacted violently.[4] Small wonder. Imagine that audience engrossed in the fate of Aias, an Athenian cult figure. They have been empathizing with him to his bitter end. The air is still resonant with the stunning poetry of Aias's death, when suddenly—in an extraordinarily irruptive entrance—the long-absent Teukros straggles in too late to save the day. Yet more unsettling, Teukros brings with him the unbeguiled social reflexes of a fifth-century Athenian.[5] Immediately he demythifies Telamon—the legendary hero father whom Aias has spent his life trying to live up to—by exposing him as a sour, aimlessly mean old man. Teukros, like Aias, is combative and courageous, but as a 'barbarian' and a lowly archer he lacks Aias's stature. Nonetheless, in dressing down the Greek commanders he can, and does, demolish the source of their unquestioned authority. And the audience? Given the collision of once timeless myths and current realities—the jamming together of high rhetoric and muckraking plain speech—their outrage seems inevitable. Sir Francis Bacon noted that "narratives made up for the stage are neater and more elegant than true stories from history, and are the sort of thing people prefer." Sophocles' audience expected him to rework a legendary past, not challenge it with a jaundiced view from their own historical moment. Yet that's exactly what Teukros does, subjecting their mythic heritage to a perspective and concerns that are wholly contemporary, mundane, and unresolved—thereby redirecting the focus of the play away from received myth and onto the audience itself. In fifth-century Athens, the sarcasm and insults crackling the air over Aias's remains may have been more shocking than the self-contained tragedy of the mythic Aias. Some spectators, especially aristocratic and oligarchic ones, must have felt unease at Teukros's open contempt for the two kings.[6] Others had to have been thrilled at the over-the-top rendering of Menelaos, the authoritarian Spartan king whom more than a few Athenian farmers, tradesmen, and warriors must have loved to hate. All we know for certain is that what that audience experienced was not 'tragedy' as might be expected—nor what a modern audience viewing tragedy through a generalized Aristotelian lens would be looking for—but a different *kind* of experience: a fundamentally civic, political, ethos-challenging drama.

The shift from an aristocratic, heroic ethos to a democratic one—tested and threatened though that might be—would seem to suggest an overall 'narrative of progress.' Yet there is none. Within the heroic ethos, Tekmessa, despite occasional checks, speaks with authority. Her noble lineage, her wife/concubine relation to Aias, and her own *sôphrosunê*, certified by the Chorus, earn her that freedom. In the relatively democratic air that seems to sweep in with Teukros, however, she's mute. She must defend Aias's remains as her child Eurysakes does; they are two speechless suppliants shielding his body with their own. What power they presume inheres, now, in their piety. Yet the social disjunct is so striking we may be reminded that in fifth-century Athens, where participation in the democratic polity was restricted, women did not have a public voice linked to political power.

The intrepid Teukros has humanizing depths and resonances of his own, however. He knows something about mentoring that Aias had no way to envision. Organizing the funeral procession, Teukros says to the still speechless Eurysakes: "You too, boy, with what strength you / can muster, and with love, put your hand / on him and help me, I need your help / to lift your father's body . . ." (1595–1598). That Eurysakes' help is more symbolic than actual doesn't make it any less crucial. In contrast, all Aias himself had imagined, by way of training or nurturing, was putting his boy's hand into the loop of the monster shield that he alone, a giant of a warrior, could bear the weight of. Short of that, the most Aias could conceive of was the play world of a child who knows neither joy nor grief— a sentimental projection steeped in the pathos of Aias's own doomed life.

The end Sophocles envisions is neither judgment nor justification, praise nor blame, but a social/political modus vivendi. Nothing could be simpler, yet harder, to achieve, though something of an answer does come from Odysseus when he feels pity for the deluded, blood-smeared Aias, despite the fact that Aias has tried to kill him. Later, the dead Aias no longer a threat, Odysseus again emphasizes that their commonality as human beings, whose lives are as "shadows in passing," runs deeper than personal differences or antagonisms.[7] Consequently, when Agamemnon grasps at reasons to prevent Aias's burial, Odysseus brushes them aside. He won't bargain that commonality away. Assuming the authority vested in him by the award of Achilles' armor, Odysseus says to Agamemnon: "However you put it [explain it, justify it], you'll do what is right" (1553). Though diplomatically posed as a statement of fact, in context this has the force of a warning. 'Right' means not what is expedient, but what human beings as human beings ought to do. "One day," Odysseus says, "I will have the same need" (1549), thus presuming a socially vested self-interest.

How might this outlook translate into our own world? It was said by Irishman John O'Leary, who had reason to say it: "There are things a man must not do to save a nation."[8]

A nation (a society, a culture, a tribe, an army, a *polis*) must have some basis in universally applicable principle; otherwise it's a pit of expediency. Some things are sacred, we say, meaning there are acts one must not commit: like torture. More horrific than 'murdering' defenseless domestic animals, as Aias does, is torturing them, which he also does. More issues and realities are aired in *Aias* than are raised here. Let's just say the play in its entirety hovers uneasily over grounds such as these, grounds no less sacred in this world than in that of fifth-century Greece.

## NOTES

**1.** The palpable disorientation of the Chorus's search parties, looking to save Aias from himself, is prefigured by the play's opening scene, which has been characterized as "a most unusual dumb show" (Taplin, 40; Hesk, 41). Greek tragedies do not begin as pantomime. Nonetheless, there's Odysseus, in the obscure stillness of early morning, trying to distinguish Aias's tracks from a muddle of others—looking not to save Aias but to ascertain if he really is the warrior, as suspected, who has slaughtered the livestock, the unsorted war spoil, that is (was) the common property of the entire Greek army.

**2.** "If we may paraphrase a famous quotation from Shelley and turn it on its head, early Greek poets from Homer (*c.* 700) to Pindar (518–446) were the 'acknowledged legislators of the word.' They were not just arbiters of elegance and taste but articulators, often controversially so, of ideologies and moral values. . . . A very special class of poets is constituted by the writers of Athenian tragedy. . . . Theirs could be an explicitly didactic genre though necessarily an indirect, analogical medium for commenting on current political affairs or ideas, since with very rare exceptions tragedy's plots were taken ultimately from the 'mythical' past of gods and heroes." —Paul Cartledge, *Ancient Greek Political Thought in Practice*

"The fifth century Athenians . . . considered the problem of the state and the basis of its authority . . . These things were discussed and debated both before and after the coming of the sophists; and we catch echoes of these debates in great literature—in Herodotus, naturally, and in the speeches of Thucydides, but also in the *Eumenides* of Aeschylus, the *Antigone* of Sophocles. It could be that the *Ajax* [*Aias*] is an important document for a transitional period of Greek thought." —R. P. Winnington-Ingram, *Sophocles: An Interpretation*

3. This "incompletely democratized culture" that did not extend to women or metics ('resident aliens' and their descendants) was nonetheless more effectively democratic than any modern democracy. The *dêmos*, the common people, had something of a handle or grip (*kratos*) on power, not least because their political engagement was relatively hands-on—actively participatory, rather than mediated through layers of putative representatives, though in time their democracy, like ours, also functioned as an empire.

4. Herbert Golder, *Introduction to Aias* (Oxford University Press, 1999, 19).

5. As a barbarian, an outsider, Teukros looks on heroic Greek self-mythification with a colder, more realistic eye than most 'natives' might be predisposed to. In certain respects this applies as well to Tekmessa, another barbarian.

6. Though Menelaos and Agamemnon are brother kings sharing command of the Greek forces, Sophocles goes out of his way to cast them in distinct political roles: Menelaos, though noble, expounds an oligarchic politic, whereas Agamemnon, the superior of the two, bases

his authority on his spectacularly sordid 'noble' lineage. (As the fifth century wore on, antidemocratic opposition coming from those of noble birth was taken up, increasingly, by the oligarchs—landowners who were not *aristoi* but who wanted special privileges in a polity of 'rule by the few.' Some strategically minded oligarchs would also try to make common cause with the *dêmos* against the nobles.) For the most part, democracy was not called *dêmokratia*, which could mean anything from "people power" to "mob rule." To forestall negative interpretations, the defenders of democracy preferred to call it *isonomia*, "equality before or under the law."

7. Greek ethos held that one must 'help friends, harm enemies.' Sophocles challenges this not only through Odysseus but through Aias himself, who concludes, with strikingly disabused *sôphrosunê*, that friends and enemies change over time. "I know, now, to hate my enemy / as one who may later be a friend. / My friend I'll help out just enough— / he may, one day, be my enemy" (829–832). Ironically, Odysseus and Aias together constitute a formidable critique of what was, even in fifth-century Athens, a seemingly unchallengeable ethos.

8. John O'Leary (1830–1907). An early member of the Irish Republican Brotherhood and editor of *The Irish People*. Imprisoned for nine years by the British, after which he went into exile in Paris. Praised by W. B. Yeats for his "moral genius," in particular because O'Leary would not allow any special pleading about the needs of a nation (i.e., the need to establish a free Irish state) to blur the outlines of good and bad, whether in action or in literature.

# Aias

*Coast of Troy. Murmurous surf. In the obscure silence of early morning,
ODYSSEUS is tracking, pausing over, footprints in the sand. Behind him
the peak of a tent, made of hides, shows above the gated walls of AIAS 's
compound.*

**VOICE OF ATHENA**

Odysseus! Every time I see you
    you're out! getting
the jump on your enemies.

*ATHENA appears. ODYSSEUS hears but cannot see her.*

Now you're nosing around the tents
Aias and his sailors pitched
here, at the edge of the sea
where all is saved or lost.
          You're looking to see
which tracks are *really* fresh,
whether he's in there or still                                    10
out here somewhere.
Well, go no further. Your nose
like a Spartan foxhound's
has led you to the right place.

You needn't sneak around to see
what's up. He's in there all right,
dripping sweat and blood spatter
          from his head
and his sword-slashing hands.

Speak. Why are you after him?                                    20
You might learn something
from one who knows.

**ODYSSEUS**
Athena? Really? No god
comes nearer my heart than you!
I can't see you but in my mind
I know you, your voice
sounds *through* me

like a bronze-mouthed trumpet!
You're right. I've been closing in
on an enemy: Aias　　　　　　　　　　　　　　30
with his monster shield.
It's he, and no other, I'm tracking.
Last night he did something unthinkable.
Or maybe he did. I'm not sure.
We're all still confused.
　　　　　I took it on myself
to get to the bottom of this.


Just now at dawn we found
all our war spoil: cattle, sheep, oxen,
even the herdsmen guarding them,　　　　　　40
butchered! Every last one.
We all think we see in this
the heavy hand of Aias.
Someone saw him charging across
the field, all by himself, swinging
his sword spraying blood.
A lookout reported this to me.
Right away I picked up the trail.
Still, the tracks are mucked up.
Some are his. The rest,　　　　　　　　　　50
who knows?


You got here just in time.
I've always counted on you
to set me straight.

**ATHENA**

Odysseus, don't I know that?
        For some time now
I've been keeping an eye out,
helping you along.


**ODYSSEUS**

I'm on the right track then?


**ATHENA**

Absolutely. He did it.                                         60


**ODYSSEUS**

It's crazy. What got into him
he'd do a thing like that?


**ATHENA**

        MAD!
He felt *he* should be awarded
the armor of Achilles.


**ODYSSEUS**

But why take it out on *animals*?


**ATHENA**

He thought the blood smearing his hands
was *your* blood.


**ODYSSEUS**

This was murder meant for *us*?

**ATHENA**

He'd have gotten you, too,                                          70
if I hadn't been watching out.

**ODYSSEUS**

How did he dare think
he'd get away with it?

**ATHENA**

By coming up on you
alone, under cover of darkness.

**ODYSSEUS**

How close did he get?

**ATHENA**

Near as the flaps
on your commanders' tents.

**ODYSSEUS**

So close? And bloodthirsty?
What stopped him?                                                  80

**ATHENA**

*I* did! I took his own
rush of horrible joy
*it was incurable*
and spun him round in it!
He couldn't see straight,
hacking at cattle, at sheep,

in the milling pool
of unsorted war spoil, cracking
spines in a widening apron
of blood and carcasses.                                              90
He thought he'd grabbed
with his own hands
the sons of Atreus—and plunged on
slaughtering one warlord after another,
me drawing him on, entangling him
deeper in misery.

He broke off then, arm weary.
The cattle and sheep still alive
he roped together and hauled
back to his camp here                                              100
as though they were men! not
beasts with horns and hooves.

He's in there now, torturing them.
See this sickness for yourself.
Then you may tell the Greeks
what you have witnessed.

*ODYSSEUS looks to slip away.*

Wait! right . . . there.
He can't hurt you now.
I'll make sure the light of his eye
won't find you.                                              110

YOU IN THERE, AIAS! Stop
hog-tying your captives.
Come out here!

ODYSSEUS
Athena, what are you *doing*! Don't.

ATHENA
Shsh! You want to be called a coward?

ODYSSEUS
God no. Just . . . let him be.

ATHENA
Why? He's the same man he was, isn't he?

ODYSSEUS
Exactly. And still my enemy.

ATHENA
*(teasing, testing)*
To gloat over your enemy,
what could be sweeter?                                      120

ODYSSEUS
I'm happy just letting him stay there.

ATHENA
Afraid to look a madman in the eye?

**ODYSSEUS**

If he wasn't mad, I would. Face him.


**ATHENA**

You could stick your face in his
he still wouldn't see you.


**ODYSSEUS**

Why not? He still sees with the same eyes.


**ATHENA**

Open and shining as they are
I'll darken them.


**ODYSSEUS**

Gods make anything the way they want.


**ATHENA**

Quiet then. Don't move.                                    130


**ODYSSEUS**

I have a choice? I wish
I were somewhere else.


**ATHENA**

AIAS! Still don't hear me?
ME!? Your comrade-in-arms!


*AIAS comes out: blood-smeared, bloody whip in hand.*

*ATHENA, invisible to ODYSSEUS, is visible to AIAS. ODYSSEUS, in turn, is invisible to AIAS.*

**AIAS**

Greetings, Athena, daughter of Zeus!
You've backed me to the hilt
and yes! on your temple I will hang
trophies of solid gold!

**ATHENA**

      That's . . . nice.
But tell me: you plunged your sword                    140
deep into the blood of the Greek army?

**AIAS**

That I did. I don't mind saying.

**ATHENA**

And drove your spear into the sons of Atreus?

**AIAS**

Never again will those two
dishonor Aias.

**ATHENA**

You mean they're dead.

**AIAS**

Yes, dead! That's the last time
they'll rob *me* of Achilles' armor.

**ATHENA**

I see. And Laertes' son, Odysseus,
what about him? He got away?                                    150


**AIAS**

That foxfucker you ask *me*
about *him*?


**ATHENA**

Yes. Odysseus. The one who's always
standing in your way.


**AIAS**

Hah! My lady, of all my prisoners,
he's *the* best. In there in chains.
I'm keeping him alive, for now.


**ATHENA**

For what? What more can you want?


**AIAS**

First I'll chain him to a post . . .


**ATHENA**

Poor man! Then what?                                    160


**AIAS**

. . . whip the living skin off his back.
*Then* kill him.

ATHENA

Torture? Do you really have to?

AIAS

Anything else, Athena, you'd have your way.
But *that* one gets what's coming to him.

ATHENA

Well, whatever pleases you,
do it.

AIAS

Right. I've work to do. But
you, be sure to watch my back
the way you did last night.                    170

*AIAS goes back inside the camp compound.*

ATHENA

You see, Odysseus, how powerful
the gods are? Have you ever known
a man more prudent, yet readier
to step up in a crisis?

ODYSSEUS

Never. Yet I feel his wretchedness.
My enemy, yes, but caught up
in a terrible doom. My doom, too.
I see that now. All we who live, live
as ghosts of ourselves. Shadows in passing.

**ATHENA**

Then think on that, and watch yourself.                    180
*Never* challenge the gods. Don't
puff yourself up when you beat someone
at something, or when your wealth piles up.
In the scale of things, one day lifts
humans up, another brings them down.
The gods love those who take care
but abhor those who cross them.

*ATHENA vanishes. ODYSSEUS leaves. The CHORUS comes on, agitated.*

**LEADER**

Son of Telamon, rock of Salamis
towering up from the crashing sea,
        when you do well                                  190
our hearts surge with joy—
but when Zeus comes down on you,
when Greek rumors come after you,
        we're flustered, like doves
with a quick, scared look!

**CHORUS**

*(severally)*

Loud whispers from the dying night
        shame us. They say you tore
across the meadow through sheep
and cattle, the horses
        wild-eyed, panicked!                              200

as you with your flashing sword
slaughtered the unsorted war spoil of the Greeks.


These whispers Odysseus
        slips into everyone's ear.
And they believe him! Each one who hears
makes more of it than the one before. It's all
        too believable! They're getting a belly laugh
making a mockery of you.


Sure. Set sights on the man who's bigger than life,
        you can't miss.                                    210
But say stuff about me, who'd listen?


It's only the great they envy after.
Yet we, down here, can't all by ourselves
like a tower
        defend the walls of a city.
We're better off working with them: the great
depend on us, we depend
on one another.


But fools too thick to learn these truths
understand nothing, they go *on* about you—          220
        what can *we* say
unless you back us up?

LEADER

Out of your sight they chatter like a flock
of noisy little birds—but if you'd just
show yourself! then
                as when the huge
bearded vulture shadows them
suddenly
they'd shrink away. And shut up.


CHORUS
(severally)
That *mother* of a rumor                              230
        shames us!
Was it Artemis riding a bull
—or what—
        drove you against
cattle that belonged to everyone?
She helped you win some victory
        or take down a stag
and you gave nothing back?
Or has the bronze-armored War God
you fought side-by-side with                          240
        as if he didn't exist
schemed against you in the night?


Aias, in your own right mind
you'd never go so far astray
you'd attack a bunch of cattle.
        It could be

the gods deranged you. But if so
may Zeus and Apollo run these rumors off.

Or if the god-almighty kings are spreading lies
or the bastard son of that hopeless race of Sisyphos          250
    Odysseus is hissing insinuations
don't sit and sit there brooding in your tent
backed against the sea: call them on it!

**LEADER**

Stand up for yourself!
You've been holed up too long,
    battle fatigued.
Out here the flames of your ruin
lick at the very heavens.
The arrogance of your enemies
    is a wind-whipped firestorm          260
roaring, tongues run amok with insults
and mockery, while we're stuck
in anguish here.

*TEKMESSA emerges from the compound. The gate is left open, exposing the tent front with its flaps closed.*

**TEKMESSA**

Shipmates of Aias, blood brothers of Athens,
you who cherish the house of Telamon
    so far away—
*now* is time for grief! Aias our rock,

our savage giant of a man gritting out everything
is down, dumbstruck. A raging
storm roils his mind!                                           270


**LEADER**

Day is backbreaking enough.
                    And night was worse?
O daughter of the Phrygian Teleutas,
by war he brought you to bed
and has loved you ever since—
          you must know
something you could tell us.


**TEKMESSA**

How speak the unspeakable?
Madness in the night gripped him
          like death—                                           280
the glory of our great Aias
          it's gone!
There . . . awful things in there.
Carcass corpses, blood-drenched offerings
by his own hand slaughtered!


**CHORUS**
*(severally)*
The way you talk about this fire-hardened warrior
we can't stand it!
               Or get past it.
With Greeks spreading the same rumor

this looms *huge*.                                         290
I dread what's next. If his crazed hand
    his dark gleaming sword
slaughtered all together, the cattle with the men
       riding herd on them
he'll die, for all to see, in shame.


**TEKMESSA**

So that's where he got them!
Some he drags in, slams down,
    cuts their throats.
Others he breaks their backs.
Then he goes after two white-footed rams,        300
cuts the head off one, then
    the tip of its tongue.
And throws it all away!
The other he ties to a pillar
upright, the forefeet up,
grabs a leather harness, doubles it
    and lashes out.
The whip hisses, he's screaming
    curses so awful
no man could think them.                          310
It must be a god
came wailing *through* him.


**CHORUS**

*(severally)*

Time to pull something over our heads

and steal away quick afoot
    or by ship
on benches pulling on banks of oars
        go . . . *some*where!
The sons of Atreus so threaten us
we could be stoned to death
    *with* him                                    320
—caught out in *his* fate—
if we stand by him.


TEKMESSA

No that's past! That lightning crash.
*Now* is soft southerly breeze
    after bloody rampage.
Now is worse harrowing pain.
He sees what he has done to himself
    all by himself—
nothing eats deeper than that.


LEADER

Then we might pull through this.                          330
Bad things seem less bad once they're over.


TEKMESSA

Would you harm your friends to lighten
your own life? Or, as a friend to friends,
share their grief?


LEADER

Lady, grief on grief is worse.

**TEKMESSA**

His madness gone, then, makes it worse.

**LEADER**

How so?

**TEKMESSA**

When he was rapt in bloody fantasy
he was happy! For us, it was horrible.
Now it's over. He's stopped, seen what he's done,                340
and dropped down in despair.
For us it's *still* horrible. Isn't this then
twice as bad?

**LEADER**

You're right. He's been struck
        by a god.
How else explain he's no happier now
than when his mind wasn't his own?

**TEKMESSA**

Exactly.

**CHORUS**

But how did this madness
        fly down on him,                                         350
tell us! We hurt too.

**TEKMESSA**

Then I'll tell you what I know.

In the dead of night, when the night-lighting
        torches had burnt out
he went for his double-edged sword
and was slipping out toward the dark
        deserted paths. For nothing.
"Aias!" I called, "what *are* you doing?
There's been no messenger, no trumpet, they're all
asleep out there!" All he said was that old                360
catchphrase: "Woman, silence
        becomes a woman."
I stopped. And said no more.


He'd already gone out alone.


What happened out there, I can't say.
He came back hauling captives
        all roped together:
bulls, sheep dogs, bleating sheep.
Some he hung upside-down
        and cut their throats.                              370
Some he broke their spine.
Still others he tied up and tortured
like they were men!


Next I know he bolts outside
talking crazy to something crossing
        his brain out there,
struggling to get the burden of his words out
cursing the sons of Atreus, and Odysseus,

all with little snorty laughs at how much
*hurt* he'd done them.                                     380


Suddenly he's tearing back in, and then . . .
            then . . .
slowly, heavily,
        he came to his senses.
And looked. At what he'd done. The blood work.
And beat at his own head, with great
        heaving sounds
sinking down—one more wreck
among the wretched carcasses of sheep.
                And sat there,                             390
fingernails digging into his hair.
A long time he didn't move. Or speak.
Then he turned. Threatened me
to tell him everything. What happened,
what had he got himself into.
My friends, I was so scared
        I told him all I knew.
And he cried! Like I never heard before!
Always he taught me only cowards
cry like that. And broken men.                             400
When he grieved it wasn't shrill
but low, rolling, like the groaning
of a wounded bull.


But now he won't move: won't eat, drink,
        just sits there

among the animals his sword butchered.
Surely he's brooding on something awful.
It's there, the way he moans his agony.
Friends, that's why I'm out here.
Go in, do something. Stop him. Sometimes                    410
when friends say something it helps.


**LEADER**

Tekmessa! From what you say
his miseries live on under his skin.


*Off: stutter babble, muted. AIAS in the tent.*


**TEKMESSA**

And worse to come. Hear it?


*AIAS, louder.*


**LEADER**

He's still mad! Or sees
what his madness has done.


**AIAS**

Son! My boy!


**TEKMESSA**

Eurysakes! He wants you!
What for? What'll I do?

**AIAS**

Teukros! Where's Teukros? Still off                    420
on raiding parties? And me dying here?

**LEADER**

Sounds sane enough. *Hey in there*
        *open up, come out!*
When he sees us, even me, he may
out of respect for our feelings
get a grip on himself.

*TEKMESSA pulls aside the tent flaps.*

**TEKMESSA**

Here. . . . See the man
and what he has done.

*AIAS exposed, steeped in his carnage.*

**AIAS**

*O O*
my sailors! friends!                                   430
    you alone
alone stand by me still—
        *look*
what a storm surge of blood wrack
breaks over & around me!

**LEADER**

You were right. Look
how far gone he is.


**AIAS**

O O
comrades, old hands
who set out with oar blades                                    440
        blazing through water—
you alone of those who care for me
can help me.
                Come!
slaughter me with these beasts!


**LEADER**

Don't say that!
Evil doesn't cure evil.
You only make it worse.


**AIAS**

        LOOK!
at the brave warrior                                    450
who did not back down—
who had the courage to murder
helpless, unsuspecting beasts.
    See me
laughed at! To my shame.

**TEKMESSA**

Please, lord, don't talk like that.


**AIAS**

Still here? Go find somewhere else!
*gods o gods*


**LEADER**

For love of the gods, ease
off. Learn something.                                    460


**AIAS**

Wretched *fate* twist! to let
  those bastards
slip through my hands, and me grab
 horned bulls, noble goats,
to pour their dark blood out.


**LEADER**

What's done is done.
Nothing can change that.


**AIAS**

 *You*
sneaking spying agent of evil,
  Odysseus! the oiliest                          470
   sleaze in the army! I know
you can't stop laughing, gloating over this.

**LEADER**

Who laughs or cries is for gods to say.


**AIAS**

Even now, broken, if I could just
set eyes on him . . . *o o o o*


**LEADER**

Don't talk so cocky. Think
what a pit you're in!


**AIAS**

O Zeus father of my line
    let me just
kill the scheming sonofabitch, his two brother-kings,          480
        and die!


**TEKMESSA**

If that's your prayer, pray my death too.
How will I live without you?


**AIAS**

                    *Aiai!*
                darkness
              is my light:
            death's shadows
        the clearest illumining
            left to me.
        O take me take me                          490

down
to live in that darkness.
I am not fit to ask
help from the gods of forever
nor goodness from men,
the creatures of a day.
Athena great goddess
torturing me
belittles me to death.
Where is a man to go?                    500
Where rest?
Where? If all my glory
mortifies among these carcasses?
Where? if mad obsessed
with victory
I disgraced myself?
A whole army gathers out there
to strike me down.


**TEKMESSA**

Don't! I can't bear hearing such a man
    speak the words                          510
he could never bring himself to speak.


**AIAS**

*Surge*
of water currents
rushing through the sea,
sea caves, sea meadows,

trees!
a long time, too long, you've kept me
here, at Troy—
but not now, not
now while I still breathe.                              520
Let everyone know that.
River Skamander, so kindly unkind
to all the Greeks: this is one soldier
whose face you won't see
float on your waters anymore.
I don't mind saying, with pride,
of all the Greek army
Troy has not seen such a warrior
as this
dishonored in the dirt of earth.                        530


CHORUS

This is horrible. What can we do?
Stop you? Let you go on? How?


AIAS

*Aiai!* My very name, Aias
is a cry in the wilderness.
Who'd have thought
my name would sound my life?
I really can cry out now
*aiai! aiai! aiai!*
my name in pieces.
I'm the man whose father won                            540
the prize of prizes, the most beautiful,

fighting here. And I'm the son
who in Troy won as much,
as powerful as he—for what, to die
in disgrace among the Greeks!

One thing for sure—had Achilles himself
lived to present his own arms
to the worthiest warrior here, I alone
would have got my hands on them. But
when the sons of Atreus procured them,                    550
giving them to that schemer who works
every angle there is—they brushed aside
all the victories of Aias!

Let me tell you something. If my eyes
my mind hadn't been seized, *hustled*
away from where they were headed,
that would've been the end of those two
lobbying the judges. Yet the stone-eyed
look of the unbending daughter of Zeus
*just as I was about to strike them*                      560
made me crazy! Stained my hands
with animal blood. Now they're out
celebrating, they got away! no thanks
to me for that. When a god spellbinds
a warrior, even losers may elude him.

                    Now what will I do?
The gods hate me. The Greeks hate me.
The very plains of Troy hate me too.

Should I abandon this beachhead, leave
the sons of Atreus to go it on their own                                    570
and sail back across the Aegean? I should
go home! Yet how can I face my father,
Telamon? How could he stand to look at me,
stripped of every shred of honor, knowing
he himself stands crowned with glory?
How could he bear it?

          Well then
should I go up to the walls of Troy
single-handed, alone, take on
every last one and go down                                                  580
fighting? But then the sons of Atreus
would be only too happy at that.

I must find a way to show my father,
old as he is, his son wasn't gutless.

To want to live
       longer, when longer
means only misery, is shameful.
What's the joy, day after day, taking
one step nearer, one step back from, death?
I figure the man who keeps on going                                         590
in hopeless hope isn't worth a damn.
If he's noble he'll live with honor
or die with it. That's all there is to it.

**LEADER**

Aias, no one says you're doing anything
but telling the truth. The way you feel it.
But hold on. Give your friends
a say in this.


**TEKMESSA**

My lord, nothing is worse than bad luck
that dooms us. My father in Phrygia
was a free man, rich and powerful,                        600
yet I'm a slave. It seems that
what the gods called for
your strong hand made happen.
Even so, now that I share your bed
I wish you well—and I beg you
by Zeus who guards our hearth,
don't leave me to your enemies'
contempt, don't let them get
their hands on me!


The day you die, I'm alone.                                610
Helpless. The Greeks
will drag me off, your son too,
to eat whatever a slave eats.
My master, *one* of my masters,
will pelt me with shame
in a hail of stinging words:
*"Look at her. Aias's whore.*
*He was such a big hero,*

*she had it so good. Now look:*
*all she does is shitwork."*                                    620
They'll say that. That's how some
demon will get on me. But think
how shameful their words leave *you*
and yours . . .

          Don't do this
to your father, so painfully aged!
Don't! Not to your mother,
so old after so many years
praying night after night
you'll come home alive.                                    630
          Pity your son
who will pass his life without you,
brought up under the thumb
of guardians who couldn't care less.
       Think what
desolate life you're leaving us.
All I have is you. With nowhere
to turn to. Backed by fate your spear
drove through my country and left it
         *gone!*                                    640
My father too, and mother, fate took
down into Hades. What home have I
without you? What means to live?
       You're my life!
Remember me? Haven't we had joy?
A man shouldn't forget that.

One kindness breeds more kindness.
But when a man lets slip away the joy
he's had, there's nothing noble in that.


**LEADER**

If only you would pity her, Aias,                    650
as I do, you'd commend what she says.


**AIAS**

Sure. I'll commend her—if
she does what I tell her to.


**TEKMESSA**

Aias, I will always do anything for you.


**AIAS**

Bring me my son. Now. I want to see him.


**TEKMESSA**

O. Yes, but . . . I was so afraid
I let him leave the tent.


**AIAS**

When I had that . . . problem? Or what?


**TEKMESSA**

Yes. In case he ran into you. And died.

**AIAS**

The way *my* fate goes, could be.                    660


**TEKMESSA**

Well, at least I stopped *that*.


**AIAS**

And you did well . . . thinking ahead that way.


**TEKMESSA**

*(stalling)*

Now, how else can I help you?


**AIAS**

I want to speak to him. Face to face.


**TEKMESSA**

Yes. Servants are watching him. Near here.


**AIAS**

Then why *isn't* he here?


**TEKMESSA**

Eurysakes! Your father's calling.
Whoever's got him, bring him here.


**AIAS**

Not coming? Can't hear you?

**TEKMESSA**

They're coming! The servant . . . here they are!                    670

*Servant brings in boy, who holds back.*

**AIAS**

Here! Up, up! Into my arms!
*(impatient, waving the servant forward)*
Fresh blood won't scare him, not if
he's truly my son. Like a colt
he has to be broken in early on
to become as his father—trained
in the savage discipline of a warrior
so that that becomes his nature.

*The boy is in his arms.*

              Dear boy
may you be luckier than I was. If so, if
you're still like me, you won't do badly.                        680
For now, I envy you your innocence.
You know nothing of evil. Life is sweetest
before we realize the joy of it, and the grief.
Then it will be up to you, to show
your father's enemies what you're made of
and whose son you are.

But for now, O, graze
on the fizzy air, be a child, a joy
to your mother here. And don't worry.

The Greeks won't dare                                690
touch you, or shame you, not
even when I'm gone. I'll leave
Teukros to watch out for you
and bring you along,
he won't let you down

. . . except, he's far away now
hunting down our enemies.

But you, my sea warriors, comrades,
you must care for him too!
Tell Teukros it is my command                        700
he take the boy back home
where he may see, and be seen by, Telamon
        and my mother, Ereboia,
to ease them in old age as they go down
into the kingdom of darkness.
And tell Teukros my weapons are not
prizes to be handed out by judges
at war games—not for the Greeks,
not for the one who is destroying me!

*(to EURYSAKES)*

Look, this is for you, Eurysakes,                    710
this shield gave you your name.
Take it. There's *seven* layers of oxhide,
no spear can pierce it. Here, grab hold
by the braided leather loop. Like so.

The other arms and armor will be
buried with me.
*(to TEKMESSA)*
Quick. Take the child inside.
Batten everything down. No crying!
Women are always doing that.
Shut the opening, *now*!                                720
A wise doctor doesn't chant prayers
when the only cure is the knife.


**LEADER**

Why the mad rush? I don't like this.
Your words are too edgy.


**TEKMESSA**

Aias, my lord, what are you thinking to do?


**AIAS**

Don't ask. Just, get hold of yourself.


**TEKMESSA**

I'm petrified! For the gods' sake,
for your child, don't leave us!


**AIAS**

Don't worry at me! Don't you know
I no longer owe the gods anything.                       730

**TEKMESSA**
Please! Don't say that!

**AIAS**
Save your breath.

**TEKMESSA**
Won't you listen?

**AIAS**
I've heard enough.

**TEKMESSA**
Lord! I'm afraid!

**AIAS**
*(to servant, indicating the tent flaps)*
Shut them! Now!

**TEKMESSA**
For the gods, give a little!

**AIAS**
Isn't it foolish to think
you can teach me, now, to change my nature?

*The tent flaps are closed over him.* TEKMESSA *and* EURYSAKES *retreat into
the compound. The gates are pulled shut behind them.*

**LEADER**

Fabulous Salamis, you must be there    740
still
sparkling above the raging battering sea
giving all men joy, for all time—
but I these long years
camped on the grassy slopes of Ida,
I wear down
against the day I will go down
into skincrawling, unknowable Hades.

**CHORUS**

*(severally)*

Now I come to grips
with yet more grief:    750
Aias, seized by the gods
with incurable madness.
The man you sent forth in war fever
to do brave things in war
now sits it out, ruminating lonely thoughts
his friends can hardly bear.
All his heroic deeds, his honors won,
the hateful sons of Atreus
let lie *like nothings* where they've fallen.

Think of his mother, her hair    760
white with years!
When she hears how
disease has eaten his heart

she won't cry to herself
with mournful nightingale notes
*o no! o no!*
she'll howl herself
inside out! beating her hands
on her breast,
tearing her gray hair out!                    770

**LEADER**

He's better off hidden
in Hades . . . this maddened
warrior from the noblest line of warriors
who's lost touch with himself
and all he was bred for,
staggering among strange thoughts.

**CHORUS**

Wretched father,
not knowing yet!
How will you bear the shame of it,
to hear                                        780
your line, never doomed before, has ended
in Aias's ruin?

*AIAS comes out, calm, with Hektor's sword in hand. TEKMESSA and
EURYSAKES also appear.*

**AIAS**

Long rolling waves of time
bring all things to light

and plunge them down again
in utter darkness. There is
nothing that cannot happen.


Solemn oaths, willpower, go under.
Just now my mind was made up,
tempered, like hot iron plunged                                   790
into cold water. Even so I felt
the sharp edge of this same mind
soften at that woman's words.
How could I leave her
a widow? my son fatherless
among enemies . . .


                I will go down
to the cleansing pool by the great salt marsh
to wash this filth off. Get out from under
the anger Athena heaps on me. I'll find                           800
some place no one passes through.
I'll dig into the earth, bury
this sword, hateful thing,
some place no one ever sees.
Let night and Hades keep it in the dark.
From the day I was given this
by Hektor, my worst enemy, the Greeks
gave me nothing but a bad time.
It's true, the old saying: *gifts*
*from enemies bring no good.*                                     810


From now on I'll know how to

give way to the gods and how
to venerate the sons of Atreus.
They give the orders. We're bound
to obey. How could it be otherwise?
Great natural forces know their place
in the greater scheme of things. So
the snowy tracks of winter melt away
before the fruit ripening into summer.
Dark night, making its rounds, makes way          820
for the white horses of day scattering light.
Savage blasts of wind die down, so as
the groaning ocean may sleep. Great
sleep itself, overcoming all, yet lets go.
It's not *sleep* binds us forever. How can
*we* not learn limits from that vast
natural discretion?

        *I* have.
I know, now, to hate my enemy
as one who may later be a friend.          830
My friend I'll help out just enough—
he may, one day, be my enemy.
Most men never find a secure
mooring in friendship.

But . . . that will all work out.
You, woman, go in and pray the gods
all my heart desires will come to pass.

*TEKMESSA **leaves.***

And you, my friends, do me the honor
she does. When Teukros comes, tell him
to care for us. And do right by you.                        840
I will go where I am going,
but soon, perhaps, you should hear
I've come through this and found
a kind of peace.


AIAS leaves.


CHORUS

(severally)

> Ooo I've got goose bumps, I'm so flat out happy
> I could fly!
> O Pan god Pan
> show yourself,
> you who get the gods to dance,
> sweep across the sea                        850
> from the snow-swirling cliffs of Kyllene,
> teach me, dance me
> the wild crazy steps of Mysia
> and Crete
> you all by yourself taught yourself—
> now I want to dance!
> And Apollo, lord of Delos, cross over
> the waters of Ikaros,
> kindly join me
> that I may see, face to face, your brilliance!        860


> Ares dissolves his blood-dark threat!

Zeus god Zeus
now in broad daylight our swift ships
can put to sea again!
Aias buries his pain
and goes, in good faith,
to make the sacrifice the gods require.


**LEADER**

Time darkens all things
and time rekindles them.
I believe anything is possible                                          870
now Aias no longer
feuds with, nor hates,
the sons of Atreus.


*MESSENGER arrives.*


**MESSENGER**

Friends! News! Teukros
is just back from Mysia. In camp,
by the generals' tent. He was
confronted by everybody at once.
The Greeks saw him coming
from way off. When he got near
they surrounded him, shouting insults,                                  880
things like *he's related to a crazy,*
*a traitor*—no way could he save himself
from being stoned to shreds. Suddenly
swords were out. In hand. But then
when it got to the breaking point

the elders broke it up. Everyone
calmed down. But where's Aias?
He's the one who needs to hear this.

**LEADER**

Just left. He's pulled himself together
with a whole new sense of purpose.                          890

**MESSENGER**

NO!! . . . I was sent too late
or took too long getting here.

**LEADER**

You've done your duty, haven't you?

**MESSENGER**

He wasn't to be let go out.
Not till Teukros gets here.

**LEADER**

          Well I'm telling you
he's gone with the best intentions
to do the best he *could* do:
make his peace with the gods.

**MESSENGER**

That's a dumb thing to say—if there's any          900
truth in what Kalchas predicted.

**LEADER**

A prophecy? What *more* do you know?


**MESSENGER**

I know what I heard. I was there.
Some chiefs were gathered around
in conference. Kalchas got up and came
over to Teukros—gave him his hand
and steered him away, out of earshot
of the generals. He insisted Aias
be kept indoors the rest of this day,
otherwise Teukros would never see him                    910
see the end of it. Kalchas himself said this.
As for Athena, her anger would end
when this day did.

           He also said,
"The gods have it in for men too
full of themselves, their bodies gotten
too big and stupid—they're only human
but think they're superhuman. Against
them, the gods are pitiless."


        His own father warned him                    920
the day he left home. Reckless Aias
rushing to war. "With your spear
go," he said, "for victory! but always
only with help from the gods."
Yet Aias was cocky. Like a fool he said:

"O father, with help from the gods
a nothing could rack up victories!
I can do it without them." He *said* that.

Another time Athena was after him
to counterattack the Trojans. Bloody them.                930
He uttered, then, words too
awful to speak: "My Lady,
go, back up the other Greeks.
Where Aias stands the battle line
will not be broken through."
That did it. Brought down on him
what no one wants: the fury of Athena.
Still, if he can get through this day
with Apollo's help, we might yet
save him. So Kalchas said.                                940

Teukros got right up and sent me
here with these orders for you.
But if he's gone, he's gone for good,
or Kalchas is no prophet.

**LEADER**
*(at the compound gate)*
Tekmessa! whose life is misery!
Come hear what this man says.
It cuts too close for comfort.

*TEKMESSA comes out with EURYSAKES.*

**TEKMESSA**

Haven't I had enough? Why get me out here
again—just as I was finding some relief?


**LEADER**

Listen. I'm afraid                                                    950
this man has news of Aias.


**TEKMESSA**

You, man, out with it. Surely not . . . the worst?


**MESSENGER**

For *you* I don't know. I'm afraid
for Aias. Has he gone out?


**TEKMESSA**

Out, yes. Why? Why scare me like this?


**MESSENGER**

Orders from Teukros: this one day
keep Aias in his tent. Don't let him
go out alone.


**TEKMESSA**

Where's Teukros? Why does he say this?


**MESSENGER**

He just got back. He believes                                         960
if Aias goes out today, he'll die.

**TEKMESSA**

No! Where did he hear this?

**MESSENGER**

From Kalchas. The seer. He fears
today, for Aias, it's life or death.

**TEKMESSA**

*AI!!* Stand, friends, between me and what
follows this foul relentless luck!
You, hurry, go meet Teukros.
The rest split up, east and west, to the far
reaches of the bay. Pick up his tracks.
He deceived me. I see that now.                          970
What love he had for me
he's thrown away. My child,
what am I to do? I can't just sit here.
I'll go too, long as I'm strong enough.
Everyone, let's go! We've no time to lose
finding this man who's in a rush to die.

**CHORUS**

We're gone almost before the words
are out of your mouth.

*CHORUS goes off in two parties. Servant takes EURYSAKES elsewhere. AIAS
on a desolate shore. A sword point sticks up from behind bushes.*

AIAS

This *killer* is set
to do what it does best.                                        980
If there were time to think
I'd think this the gift
of Hektor, the guest-friend
I hated most the sight of—
sticking up from the enemy earth
of Troy, its edge
fresh off the grinding stone.
I've embedded it with care
for a quick, merciful death.

I have done all I can do.                                       990
Now it's up to you, Zeus,
as it should be, to help me.
I ask little enough, just
a messenger to break the news
to Teukros—to be the first to pull
me up off the blood-running sword
before my enemies come running
to throw my body to the dogs
and crows. That's all I ask of you.

        From Hermes,                                            1000
who takes us under, I ask only
a short quick death, a soundless leap
from waking to sleep, as the sword
slips through me.

I call also
on the deathless virgins who see
all human suffering: the dread
        ever-overtaking Furies.
Look how the sons of Atreus
have brought my life to a rotten end!                    1010
Overcome their vile lives with vile deaths!
O Furies, let your rage drink the blood
of the whole body of the Greek army!


        And you there,
Helios, chariot wheels climbing the sky,
as you pass over my homeland
pull up on your gold shimmering reins,
tell my death, my disaster, to my father
so old now, and to the luckless woman
who suckled me. Poor mother!                             1020
When she hears this her wailing
will overwhelm the city. But now's
no time for tears. Time now is only
to do, and quickly.


        Death, Death! look at me!
We will have words in the otherworld.
And Helios, bright day, this is the last
I will see of you. Not ever again!
O light! O holy Salamis, hearth
of my fathers, and great Athens too                      1030
whose people grew up with mine,

and the springs and rivers, the very
plains of Troy, good-bye to all
who have nursed me in this life.


This is the last word Aias has
for you. The rest I will speak
only to the dead in Hades.


*AIAS falls on his sword. His body is screened by the bushes. CHORUS in two
parties—"hurried and disorderly" (Garvie, 209)—stumble in from opposite
directions.*


**SEMI-CHORUS 1**

> Take pains, get pain,
> pain piled on.
> Where haven't I looked?                    1040
> Where have I?
> Still no sign anywhere.
> Listen! What's that?


**SEMI-CHORUS 2**

> Your shipmates!


**SEMI-CHORUS 1**

> What's the word?


**SEMI-CHORUS 2**

> We've covered the west.

**SEMI-CHORUS 1**

And . . . ?

**SEMI-CHORUS 2**

Nothing. Hard going.

**SEMI-CHORUS 1**

Nothing on the road from where the sun comes, either.

**CHORUS**

*(severally)*

If only some fisherman      1050
out fishing day and night,
or nymph from Olympus or some
stream rushing toward the Bosphoros
could shout to us they've seen
somewhere
a man of ferocious heart wandering through!

It's hard making my way
aimless,
no wind at my back,
to catch a glimpse of that fast fading man.      1060

*Off: short, sharp scream.*

**CHORUS**

From the wood! Who screamed?

*Off: drawn-out howl.*

*Disclosure of TEKMESSA, rising from behind the bushes that hide the body of AIAS. Two parties of the CHORUS converge.*

**CHORUS**
*(severally)*
Tekmessa!
        His spear-gotten bride . . .
dissolved in her own cries.

**TEKMESSA**
Now nothing . . . left! I'm lost! My friends . . .

**CHORUS**
What?

**TEKMESSA**
Here. Aias. Fresh slaughter.
His sword buried in his body.

**CHORUS**
*(severally)*
                    Nooo! We'll never get home!
                        Lord you've killed us too,                    1070
                    your own comrades! And you,
                        poor woman.

**TEKMESSA**
*AIAI!* his very name, Aias, cries out of us!

**LEADER**

Who had a hand in this?

**TEKMESSA**

Himself alone. *He* planted the sword
he fell on. The sword stands witness.

**CHORUS**

*(severally)*

And I saw nothing!
Blind, dumb, and you by your own hand
in your own blood
with no friends to watch over you!                1080
Where now is Aias
relentless as the grief sounding his name?

*TEKMESSA covers the corpse with a robe.*

**TEKMESSA**

Don't look! I'll wrap him
in my robe. Nothing must show.
None who loved him could bear seeing
the blood gasping up through his nostrils,
darkening from the wound
his own hand opened.

Now what will I do?
Who'll lift you up? Where's Teukros?                1090
If he would just come, give

composure to his brother's corpse!
O Aias, to have from so high
come to this! Even your enemies
must to their sorrow feel it.


**LEADER**

It had to be, had to,
you were so thick-hearted
you had to push your fate to the bitter end.
All night long,
all day, you'd be groaning,                                    1100
raging at the sons of Atreus
with inextinguishable murder in your heart.
Yes, the day
Achilles' arms became a contest prize
for the best warrior,
that day began this misery.


*TEKMESSA groans.*


**LEADER**

Grief this deep stops the heart.


*TEKMESSA, howling.*


**LEADER**

I don't
wonder you cry out over and over,
you've lost so much.                                          1110

**TEKMESSA**

You imagine my life. I live it.

**LEADER**

Yes.

**TEKMESSA**

Ah child, our new overseers will put
the collar of slaves on us.

**CHORUS**

>       *Shsh!* It's unspeakable
>      how brutal the sons of Atreus
>        will be to you in your grief.
>          Pray the gods stop them!

**TEKMESSA**

Yet the gods had a hand in this.

**LEADER**

The gods' burden will break us.                            1120

**TEKMESSA**

Athena, dread daughter of Zeus,
she concocted this. She'll do
anything for her Odysseus.

**CHORUS**

>       Sure in the darkness of his heart
>          that long-calculating man

has to be thrilled!
He mocks this mad frenzy,
he laughs, and with him
the sons of Atreus have a good laugh too.


**TEKMESSA**

Then let them laugh! *Joy* in his sorrows.                    1130
They didn't miss him alive? Maybe they will
when in the thick of it they find he's gone!
Men with no sense don't know what good
they have . . . till they've thrown it away.

His death leaves more pain to me
than joy to them. His own joy is
he got what he wanted. And met his own death
on his own terms. What's for them
to celebrate? His death is between him
and the gods—and not, no way, for *them*.                    1140
Let Odysseus mouth off. What was Aias
is gone. And left me wretched.


**VOICE OF TEUKROS**

*o god o god o aias o god*


**LEADER**

        Quiet!
I think I hear Teukros, shouting something
awful striking the heart of this disaster.


*TEUKROS appears.*

**TEUKROS**

Brother Aias, dear familiar face,
what I hear, is it true?

**LEADER**

He's dead, Teukros. Know that for a fact.

**TEUKROS**

    This falls on me!                                              1150

**LEADER**

That's it, for sure.

**TEUKROS**

    The rashness of it!

**LEADER**

Yes. Let it all out.

**TEUKROS**

    So *sudden* a doom . . .

**LEADER**

Sudden, yes.

**TEUKROS**

    But his son!
Where will I find him in this *Troy*?

**LEADER**

Alone. In the tent.


**TEUKROS**

     Get him. NOW!

before our enemies bag him like                    1160

a lion cub whose mother finds it gone.

Go! Hurry! Help him! Others too!

Men can't help crowing over

the dead—once they are dead.


*TEKMESSA hurries off.*


**LEADER**

While he lived, Teukros, that's exactly what

he commanded: that you watch over his son.

And you do.


**TEUKROS**

A worse sight I have not seen

in all my life—the road here

became the worst I ever walked                    1170

when I learned, Aias, it was

your death I was on the trail of.

Word of it raced through the Greek army

like a message from the gods. It got to me

before I could get to you. Hearing it I

moaned low my wretchedness. But here

now the sight of this unnerves me

    *aiai!*

*(to sailor)*

You. Uncover. Let's see the worst.

*The sailor does so, behind the screen of bushes.*

It's awful to see in the flesh                                      1180
courage this brutal. What fields of grief
your death seeds for me! Where
will I go now? Who will welcome me
who couldn't help you through this?
Naturally our father Telamon
will be all smiles when I come home
without you—that same man who,
after getting good news, is no less
sour than before. He'll curse me out
as the bastard of a captive girl, war spoil,                       1190
a coward who let you down. Or charge that
calculating to get your privilege and power
I betrayed you. Overbearing, foul-tempered,
aimlessly mean old man! He'll say all that
and banish me. His words will brand me
a *slave*. That will be my welcome home.
Now enemies are everywhere, same as
in Troy. *This* your death has left me.

Now what? How can I lift you off
the acrid glint of the swordpoint                                  1200
that took your breath away? You see

how even in death your enemy, Hektor,
took you down?
*(to sailors)*
                    Look how fate
bound these two together! With the war belt
Aias gave him, Hektor was gripped
against the chariot rails and dragged,
mangled, till his life gave out. In turn,
Aias got this gift from Hektor
and fell on it.                                        1210


                    Wasn't this sword forged
by the Furies? And that war belt by Hades,
the savage craftsman who fashions death
for everyone? As I see it, these things
and all such always are ways the gods
set men up. Anyone who sees this otherwise,
think what you like. This thought is mine.


**LEADER**
Don't drag this out. Think how you'll bury
your brother—and what will you say now
that your enemy's coming up. There!                   1220
He's the type that could mock us our loss.


**TEUKROS**
From the army? Who?

CHORUS

The Menelaos we came all this way to help.


TEUKROS

O yes. This close
there's no doubt who *he* is.


*MENELAOS arrives with guards and a herald.*


MENELAOS

Hey, you! Don't lift that corpse don't
even touch it! That's an order.


TEUKROS

A tall order. Why waste your breath on it?


MENELAOS

Because I say so. Our commander says so too.


TEUKROS

Then maybe you'd care to tell us                              1230
on what grounds you order this?


MENELAOS

We brought him here thinking
he'd be a friend, an ally of the Greeks.
He turned out to be a worse enemy
than any Trojan. With his spear he
plotted to murder us all in the night.

If a god hadn't stopped him, it would be
*our* doom now to die his shameful death,
exposed to all, while he'd still be alive.
Yet the god drove his mad rage aside                          1240
against cattle and sheep. Not a man alive
has the power, now, to bury him in a grave.
We'll haul the carcass out onto damp
yellow sands somewhere, for seabirds
to feed on. So don't puff yourself up
threatening us. We couldn't in life
keep him in line, but like it or not, in death
we will. He will go wherever our hands
take him, and leave him, seeing as in life
he never listened to a word I said.                          1250


When a common person defies his betters
it shows he's no good. What city can thrive
where there's no fear of the law? How keep
discreet order in an army camp without
shutting it up in fear and respect? Even
a man grown gigantic, he should watch it!
One little slip, he could go down. No,
the man who lives in fear and shame
is safe. But in a city of no respect, just
insolence and willfulness, though it                         1260
enjoy awhile a following wind, one day
it will go under. Fear is in order.
Why dream we can do what we want
without paying for it? One such turn

deserves another. This man flared up, all
hot-tempered and cocky. Now it's
my turn for high-and-mighty thoughts.

I warn you: bury that man, you may
bury yourself with him.

**LEADER**

You've set down right-minded precepts,                    1270
Menelaos. Don't overreach yourself
outraging the dead.

**TEUKROS**

My friends, it's no surprise that a nobody
of common stock offends, in his own way,
when a supposed noble can talk such trash.

Again now. You say you brought him here
as an ally. He didn't sail here on his own?
His own master? What justifies your claim
to command him and his men? You rule
the Spartans, not us. You've no more grounds     1280
to claim power over him than he over you.
You yourself came under orders; you're not
the commander of these forces. So how is it
you command Aias?

      Lord it over those
you're lord over. Give *them* a tongue-lashing

with your big talk. I'll bury Aias the proper way
no matter what you or that other general say.
Your mouth doesn't scare me. Aias didn't, like
those poor bastards in the ranks, come here                    1290
to get you your wife back. He came
because of an oath he'd taken. Not for you.
He wouldn't go to war for the shell of a man.
Next time you come here bring more heralds,
bring the commander in chief! Make
all the racket you want. As long as you are
what you are, I wouldn't bother to notice.


**LEADER**
Again insulting words! On top of all this?
I don't like it. Even if they *are* called for.


**MENELAOS**
The archer, far from blood dust, thinks he's something.      1300


**TEUKROS**
I'm very good at what I do.


**MENELAOS**
How you'd brag . . . had you a shield.


**TEUKROS**
Barehanded I'd match *you* in *all* your armor.

**MENELAOS**

Your courage is all in your mouth.

**TEUKROS**

A righteous cause is my courage.

**MENELAOS**

What? It's right to defend my killer?

**TEUKROS**

Your killer!? You're dead? And still alive?

**MENELAOS**

A god saved me. But he *wanted* me dead.

**TEUKROS**

If the gods saved you, why disrespect them?

**MENELAOS**

How do I disrespect the gods?                              1310

**TEUKROS**

By forbidding the burial of the dead.

**MENELAOS**

This was our enemy. It's right to forbid him rest.

**TEUKROS**

Did Aias ever *really* confront you as an enemy?

**MENELAOS**

We hated one another. You know that.


**TEUKROS**

Sure. He knew you rigged the vote against him.


**MENELAOS**

The judges made that ruling. Not me.


**TEUKROS**

You'd put a straight face on any crooked scheme.


**MENELAOS**

Talk like that could get someone hurt.


**TEUKROS**

Not us more than you.


**MENELAOS**

One last time. He will not be buried.                    1320


**TEUKROS**

I'm telling you. He will.


**MENELAOS**

I saw, once, a real blowhard make
his crew sail into a spell of bad weather.
When the storm broke, you wouldn't have heard
a peep out of him, scrunched under his robe,
not daring to breathe a word with the crew

running round stepping all over him. So
you. One little cloudburst may set off
a monster storm that will drown you out.


**TEUKROS**

Me too. I once saw a fool so full                    1330
of himself, he made fun of others' misery.
It happened a man like me, the way I feel
it could be me, said something like
"Man, don't disrespect the dead. You do,
you will pay for it." To his face said it,
the face of the fool standing before me now,
Menelaos. How's that for talking double-talk?


**MENELAOS**

I'm leaving. It would be shameful if anyone knew
I, with so much power, stooped to quibble with you.


**TEUKROS**

Then get! Shame is in standing still                 1340
blasted by hot air from a fool.


*MENELAOS and Attendants leave.*


**LEADER**

A big fight for sure. And soon.
Move, Teukros! Find a hollowed-out spot,
some moldy darkness men will hold
famous forever as his tomb.

*TEKMESSA reappears with EURYSAKES in hand.*

**TEUKROS**

Just in time, his wife and son are here
to perform the burial rites.

         You, boy, come here.
Stand by the father who gave you your life.
Press your hand on him, clutching locks of hair:                   1350
mine, your mother's, your own.
The suppliant's power that is stored there
will go under with him. And if anyone
comes from the army to pull you away,
damn him, let *him* lie unburied out
in nowhere, his people cut off at the roots
the way I cut this lock. Take it. Let no one
move you. Hold on to him. *Don't let go.*

And you, don't stand around like women
but as men! Keep close. Defend him                                 1360
until I return, after I've made a grave
for this man, no matter who forbids it.

*TEUKROS leaves.*

**CHORUS**
*(severally)*
      When, when will these wandering years
        add up to something, anything

to put an end
to this spear-driving backbreaking work
on the plains of Troy
whelmed in the shame and sorrow of the Greeks.


He should have been sucked up into the sky
or plunged into the black hole                    1370
of ever open Hades—
the man who taught Greeks
to combine forces with hateful arms
for making war,
exhaustion reviving exhaustion
to kill men.


The thrill of myrtle garland
brimming shallows of wine bowls
sweet crescendos of flutes
all that that man has taken from me,             1380
taken my sleep
and love making love into the night.
I'm left out here, who cares?
my hair sopping wet, sodden with night dew,
never to let me forget
I'm here, in miserable rotten Troy.


Was a time massive Aias held off
nightmares, and waves of arrows.
Now he is given up
to the brute demon that pursued him.             1390

Ahead

what joy can I see?

O to be blown homeward

to the wooded headland towering up

over the beating sea.

To sail! under the high

tableland of Sounion

hailing all praise to blessed Athens.


*TEUKROS returns.*


**TEUKROS**

Watch it! I hurried back seeing

Agamemnon's almost here! For sure                    1400

he'll be running off at his mindless mouth.


*AGAMEMNON enters, followed by MENELAOS and Armed Attendants.*


**AGAMEMNON**

You there! With the big mouth insulting us.

Think you'll get away with it? Yes, you.

Son of a slave. To think how you'd strut

and sound off if your mother were well-born—

nobody that you are, standing up for

something that's a nothing. And to claim

we have no authority, on land or at sea,

to command you—that Aias sailed here

as his own chief! Dangerous talk,                    1410

coming from a slave.

Your great man,
where did he go, where stand, that I did not?
Was he the only man in the Greek army?
It may be we'll regret the day we held
a contest for Achilles' armor—if Teukros
denounces us because he won't accept
the judges' decision, a clear majority,
but keeps backstabbing, tearing us down
the way lowborns do. What laws would hold up          1420
if we overruled judges, replacing the winners
with losers? This has to be stopped.
It's not the burly broad-shouldered who
come out on top, but those with brains.
A big strong ox is kept on the road
by a little whip. You may get some of that
yourself, if you don't listen to reason.
You, who are so insolent defending
a shadow man.


Get hold of yourself,                    1430
Teukros, know your place. A free man's
qualified to plead your case. Go find one.
I can't understand your barbarian babble.


**LEADER**

You should both be sensible.
That's the best I can tell you.

**TEUKROS**

*(turning his back on AGAMEMNON)*

Wonderful! That's gratitude for you. You're
dead, and gratitude has turned tail: a traitor.
This man hasn't one word to say for you
Aias, the man you fought for at spear
point . . . put your life on the line for.                                    1440
It's all gone. Tossed off.

*(wheeling round to face AGAMEMNON)*

       . . . And you!

going on and on, glib and mindless: you don't
recall backing across the ditch, falling behind
your barricades? You, down to nothing?
Aias only, all alone, came to save you!
With flames leaping up over the sterns
roiling the decks, Hektor striding the ditch
bounding over barricades toward the ships,
and who stopped him? Wasn't this the work                                     1450
of one who, you say, went nowhere but
where you went too?


       You won't admit
he served you honorably? Not when he fought
Hektor hand-to-hand? Not that he had to.
He cast his own lot into the plumed helmet.
Not wet clay that breaks up, either, but baked
hard and light, so it could rise to the top
when the helmet was shaken up.

That's who *he* was.                                             1460
And I stood with him. Me, the slave,
the son of a barbarian mother.


Where are you looking? at what?
to go on this way? You don't know
your father's father, old Pelops, was born
a Phrygian barbarian? Atreus who
fathered you fed his own brother a meal
so ghastly—his brother's own children!
Your own mother, a Cretan woman,
was caught by her own father in bed                             1470
with a slave! For that he ordered her
drowned in the silence of fishes. That's
where *you're* from. And you talk about
*my* origins? I
am the son of Telamon. My mother
is royal blood, born of Laomedon. She,
the most precious war spoil, was awarded
to Telamon by Herakles himself,
son of Alkmene. I, as the son
of two such noble parents, cannot                               1480
dishonor this man, my own blood,
who died so badly—while you, shameless
would throw his body away unburied.


Now hear this. Wherever you dump him
you'll have to dump our three bodies, too.
There's more honor dying for him

out here, for all to see, than lost in war
for your wife. Or was it your brother's wife?
Watch out! For yourself, not me.
One move toward me you'll wish                        1490
you *had* been a coward.


ODYSSEUS *arrives.*


**LEADER**

Lord Odysseus, just in time! *If* you mean
to loosen this knot, not yank it tighter.


**ODYSSEUS**

What's going on, my friends? Way back there
I could hear the sons of Atreus shouting over
this brave man's corpse.


**AGAMEMNON**

Only because, Lord Odysseus, we've been hearing
outrageous rant from this man here.


**ODYSSEUS**

Outrageous? How so? I'd make allowance
for a man who answers insults with outrage.        1500


**AGAMEMNON**

I insulted him all right. For acting against me.


**ODYSSEUS**

O? How did he wrong you?

**AGAMEMNON**

He says he won't let this corpse lie there,
he'll bury it. To defy me.

**ODYSSEUS**

As a friend, may I speak the truth
yet keep rowing in time with you?

**AGAMEMNON**

Of course. I'd be foolish to say no.
Of all the Greeks, you're my greatest friend.

**ODYSSEUS**

Listen. Keep faith with the gods. Don't,
so coldly, throw this man out exposed                    1510
naked to the world. Don't let the violence
so seize you with hate, you crush
justice under your foot. To me, too,
he was an enemy, the worst in the army,
from when I won Achilles' armor.
Yet despite that, I had to admit,
of all the Greeks who came to Troy, none
could equal him. Except Achilles.
There's no justice in disrespecting him,
you can't hurt him more—but you could                    1520
break the everlasting law of the gods.
It's horribly wrong to harm a brave man
when he's dead. However much you hate him.

**AGAMEMNON**

*You*, Odysseus? Side with him against me?

**ODYSSEUS**

I do. Yet hated him
when it was honorable to hate.

**AGAMEMNON**

Then why not step on him, now he's dead?

**ODYSSEUS**

O son of Atreus, what honor is there
gloating over such a triumph?

**AGAMEMNON**

For the ruler, it's hard to show piety.                     1530

**ODYSSEUS**

It's not hard to respect friends
who give him good advice.

**AGAMEMNON**

A loyal man defers to those who rule him.

**ODYSSEUS**

Easy now! You have the best of it
when you listen to your friends.

**AGAMEMNON**

Think what man you're standing up for!

**ODYSSEUS**

That man was my enemy. But a noble one.

**AGAMEMNON**

What's that mean? Respect a dead enemy?

**ODYSSEUS**

Yes. His greatness weighs more with me
than our enmity.                                               1540

**AGAMEMNON**

The man changes *like that*.

**ODYSSEUS**

Many men are friends. Then enemies.

**AGAMEMNON**

You approve such men as friends?

**ODYSSEUS**

I wouldn't approve an obstinate one.

**AGAMEMNON**

You'll have us looking like cowards.

**ODYSSEUS**

No. All Greeks will see us
as brave, and just.


**AGAMEMNON**

You're saying I should let them bury him.


**ODYSSEUS**

Yes. One day I will have the same need.


**AGAMEMNON**

So. In all things man works for himself.                    1550


**ODYSSEUS**

Of course. Who else?


**AGAMEMNON**

Then this will be your doing, not mine.


**ODYSSEUS**

However you put it, you'll do what is right.


**AGAMEMNON**

For you I will do this—and would do
much more, believe me. But *him*,
as in life, so in the shadows below,
I hate. Do what you want with him.


*AGAMEMNON, MENELAOS, and Armed Attendants leave.*

**LEADER**

Whoever says you weren't born wise
in your very bones, Odysseus, is a fool.

**ODYSSEUS**

If I may . . . I want to tell you                          1560
Teukros: much as I was his enemy,
now I'm ready to be his friend.
I want to help you bury the dead,
to share your concerns—do what
is necessary, and right, to honor
this towering man among men.

**TEUKROS**

Noble Odysseus, I salute you for this.
I misjudged you, completely. Of all the Greeks
his worst enemy, you were the only one
to come forward and stand up for him.                      1570
You hadn't the heart, here, to heap
the insults of the living on the dead—
unlike that mad, arrogant commander,
him and his brother, who'd filthy up
the corpse rather than bury it. For that
may Zeus, lord of Olympos, and the
unforgetting Furies, and Justice that puts
an endpoint on everything . . . doom them
to the abomination they wished on him.

Except, son of old Laertes, I'm afraid                     1580
I can't let you prepare, or touch, the body.

That might offend the dead. Help in
any other way is welcome, though.
Bring others from the Greek army.
Now I have work to do. Just know
you are, to us, a magnanimous friend.

**ODYSSEUS**

I'd wanted to help. But as that's your
wish, I understand. I will leave.

*ODYSSEUS leaves.*

**TEUKROS**

We've lost too much time. Hurry.
Some of you dig the grave, others                              1590
set the tall tripod for the caldron
over the fire, ready to heat
the holy cleansing bath. Someone else
bring his body armor from the tent.
You too, boy, with what strength you
can muster, and with love, put your hand
on him, and help me, I need your help
to lift your father's body—easy now,
the warm veins are still welling
his black blood out.                                          1600

          Come
everyone who called him friend,
hurry!

perform this service for this man
who was as noble as they come.

*Funeral procession forms.*

CHORUS
What men see, they know.
But until the future arrives
no one can see it coming
nor what is in it.

ALL *leave, carrying the body of* AIAS.

# NOTES TO THE PLAY

TEKMESSA *concubine/wife of Aias* Nominally Tekmessa is Aias's concubine, a "spear-taken" woman, but substantively she is his wife.

7 *where all is saved or lost* Literally, "the post at the end of the line." The outermost posts, being most vulnerable, are key. At Troy they were held by Achilles and by Aias.

25 *I can't see you* Athena is invisible to Odysseus, as Odysseus is invisible to Aias. Aias does see Athena, however.

28 *like a bronze-mouthed trumpet* ". . . the trumpet was invented for the Etruscans by Athena" (Garvie, 126).

151–152 *That foxfucker you ask me / about* him? The Greek *kinados* is a 'coarse' Sicilian word for fox. It is not gender specific. The epithet not only characterizes Odysseus but registers Aias's revulsion at the mere mention of his name. "Fox," in itself, carries some of the meaning but little of the weight, and even less the edge, of the original—nor do conventional qualifications such as "stinking," "cunning," "slippery," or "villainous." The key circumstance is that Aias is out of his mind, "screaming curses so awful no man could think them," as Tekmessa reports, adding that it must have been "a god came wailing *through* him" (308–312). Foxfucker has a suitably infamous *aural* lineage, the dead metaphor of "motherfucker" having metastasized into (or been metastasized from) like-sounding toxic epithets.

189 *Son of Telamon, rock of Salamis* Telamon, the father of Aias, was the first Greek warrior to scale the walls of Troy during the earlier expedition led by Herakles. Salamis is an island near Athens.

212 *only the great they envy after* "After" traces the submerged metaphor of the original Greek, where envy "creeps."

226–227 *as when the huge / bearded vulture* The Greek is "vulture." Yet vultures, as scavengers, eat only carrion, which here doesn't make sense. Some have conjectured that "most probably the Greeks made no clear distinction between vultures and eagles" (Garvie, 141–142). Others take the vulture to be a lammergeier, or bearded vulture, which is not a true vulture but a raptor. "Bearded vulture" seems sufficiently ominous—also, not likely to raise dramatically irrelevant questions as to how a scavenger could possibly threaten live Greek warriors.

230–232 *That* mother *of a rumor . . . Artemis riding a bull* Artemis Tauropolis, the bull rider, often associated with madness. Aias, as a hunter, has of course slaughtered animals, including bulls.

238 *and you gave nothing back?* Speculation that Aias may have cheated Artemis—either not giving her a share of the war spoil, or withholding her share of game he had gotten while hunting.

239 *bronze-armored War God* Ares. Speculation that Aias is being punished for not having acknowledged the help Ares gave him in battle.

284 *Carcass corpses* He has killed animals (carcasses) under the delusion that they were human beings (corpses). This gloss, of what is only implicit in the Greek, highlights the enormity of Aias's crime. The slaughter is a transgression not only of social and political order—as a Greek hero, by definition individualistic, Aias has destroyed the common property of the entire Greek army—but of the far greater natural order he will invoke later as he contemplates the bind he is in. If "Great natural forces know their place / in the greater scheme of things," he asks, why can't he do the same? (816–817)

457 *Go find somewhere else!* Literally, "Go off back again as to your foot to pasture." i.e., Go graze in some other pasture. To preclude contemporary misreadings of this idiomatic phrase (Aias is *not* dismissing Tekmessa as a metaphorical cow) the present translation cuts the line to its essence.

464 *noble goats* Literal translation. Aias, in the depths of self-degradation, has a heightened sense of the dignity of these animals. This also suggests the physical presence of goats: their stately bearing (heads held high, like lamas) and the venerable aura of their goatees.

522 *River Skamander* One of the two main rivers in the Troad, the area around Troy, which is today the northwestern part of Anatolia, Turkey.

522–523 *River Skamander, so kindly unkind / to all the Greeks* The Skamander's affective relation to the Greeks has been translated in mutually exclusive ways. Positive: (a) "so kindly to the Argives," (b) "kindly to the Greeks," (c) "Friendly Skamander / river we love!" Negative: (a) "hostile to the Greeks," (b) "inimical to the Greeks," (c) "river that hates all Greeks." Yet another translation has it that the Skamander is "kinder to other Greeks" than it is to Aias himself. The present translation joins the difference—if only because, dramatically, it makes both objective and subjective sense. The Skamander has been "kindly unkind" in that it *is* the Skamander, the river of an enemy territory the Greeks are bogged down in, and yet the river *as* river has served them in various ways, not least as drinking water. Here the Skamander is the mirror in which Aias sees, memorializes, and takes leave of himself. See also lines 1032–34: "and the springs and rivers, the very / plains of Troy, good-bye to all / who have nursed me in this life."

523 *this is one soldier* Speaking of himself in the third person, Aias already sees himself as a dead man.

533–539 Aiai! *My very name, Aias, / is a cry . . . my name in pieces* Much is made of Aias's name. Here he refers it back to *AI, AI,* the letters of lament marking the petals of the hyacinth, the flower that sprang from the blood of Hyacinthus, beloved of Apollo, when he was killed by the jealous wind god Zephyrus.

550 *procured them* He accuses Agamemnon and Menelaos of buying the votes by which Odysseus was awarded Achilles' armor.

555–556 hustled / *away from* Literally, "rushed away from." In being rushed away from his intended human targets, he has been hustled (rushed *plus* deceived, as in a scam) by Athena into attacking and destroying the war spoil of the Greeks.

558–559 *yet the stone-eyed / look of the unbending daughter of Zeus* Athena. Literally, "Gorgon-eyed." Whoever looked on the Gorgon Medusa was turned to stone. "Unbending": the Greek could read as "unconquerable" or "unwedded."

617 *Look at her. Aias's whore.* The subtext is a bitter evocation of Hektor's sensitive, nuanced family scene with Andromache and Astyanax (*Iliad*, book 6). "Tekmessa shames [Aias] by turning Homeric Hektor's note of sympathy into a sarcastic saying by one of [Aias's] enemies. [Her] bitterness is enhanced by the fact that she replaces Hektor's word 'wife' [which Andromache, unlike Tekmessa, really is] with the term 'concubine'" (Hesk, 68). 'Concubine,' now almost exclusive to Chinese period films, is too hieratic to be carried over into contemporary English. Our own social categorizations, which are not stylized, might locate a concubine somewhere between a 'partner' and a mistress. Yet neither describes Tekmessa, nor conveys the viciousness of the Greek epithet in this context where—as dramatized and realized by Tekmessa—it's not just a name but a fate. I've assumed that 'whore,' a threadbare slur in our world, serves as an appropriate breach of decorum within the ethos of *Aias*.

658 *When I had that . . . problem? Or what?* Aias and Tekmessa, usually so direct about their realities and anxieties, tread lightly when referring to Eurysakes. Neither knows how far Aias's madness might have taken him.

672–714 *Here! Up, up! Into my arms! . . . he won't let you down* In performance the sight of Eurysakes (a child named after, and destined to inherit, a shield so ponderous only Aias could wield it) may possibly have triggered a disjunction in the minds of some in the audience—especially given the presence of dead warriors' orphans, arrayed in the new hoplite armor awarded them by the polis, occupying a place of honor at the festival.

675–677 *trained / in the savage discipline . . . his nature* It's customary to translate "savage discipline" euphemistically. "Savage" becomes "rugged," "rough," or "harsh" and so loses its edge. "Discipline" settles down into "ways." But the Greek *ômos* means "savage," with all the rawness and cruelty that word implies. And what are called "ways," as though this were simply habitual, is the more purposeful *nomos*. *Nomos* could mean "ways," but the greater part of its semantic range is explicitly socially conditioned, referring to law, custom (habitual or self-consciously chosen mores), or rule. In a military context, it may refer to a discipline. That Eurysakes must be broken in, "trained" to become as his father, indicates that the warrior way of being is not simply a matter of temperament, nor something one happens to fall into. In Aias's world, one is trained in a discipline until it becomes his nature. That's why Aias can say to Tekmessa: "Isn't it foolish to think / you can teach me, now, to change my nature?" (738–739) The key word is "now."

729 *Don't worry at me!* Aias is *really* annoyed, hence the "at." Originally, "worrying" was what dogs or wolves did to sheep (from the Middle English *wirien*, to harass). In modern usage, "worry" in and of itself, without further emphasis, isn't strong enough to communicate the hair-trigger

intensity of Aias's reaction to Tekmessa's persistence in challenging him.

748 *into skincrawling, unknowable Hades* 'Skincrawling' covers two ambiguous compound epithets: one signifying 'from whom one turns away' (the 'abhorred'), the other, 'who is invisible' or, possibly, 'who makes invisible' (Garvie, 182). 'Skincrawling' attempts to consolidate the chorus leader's shudder of revulsion with the sinking of his heart at the blind prospect of Hades. Cf. note, 1.845.

783–844. *Long rolling waves of time . . . a kind of peace* Traditionally this is called the deception speech. Though technically addressed to Tekmessa and the chorus, substantively this is a monologue. It is driven not primarily by the desire to deceive, but by Aias's need to absorb the implications of his situation. Even as he ruminates on the orderliness of the natural world, the ebb and flow of power, he succeeds only in calling up a world he cannot live in. In an uncharacteristically mild manner he asks Tekmessa and the chorus to pray that "all my heart desires will come to pass." He anticipates coming through this and finding "salvation" or "deliverance"—or, as translated here, "a kind of peace."

*The deception issue.* Aias speaks the truth of his world. The calm with which he comes to terms with himself—the tautological "I will go where I am going"—has the feel of psychological truth as well (Woodruff, 51–52). That the chorus, left to their own devices, misread Aias's intention doesn't mean he has spoken to deceive them. They have a stake in deceiving themselves. In the hysteria of their anxiety to believe Aias will stay to protect them, they jump to the conclusion they are desperate for ("Ooo I've got goose bumps, I'm so flat out happy / I could fly!") even as they misinterpret it ("Aias . . . goes, in good faith, / to make the sacrifice the gods require"). To call the speech a deception is presumptive, reducing it to a function-driven act of audience (chorus) manipulation. To *realize* this extraordinary meditation we have to enter into the flow where it is simultaneously finding itself and revealing itself—each moment informing, but not presuming, the next. At every shift of phrase or association, Aias is meaning what he is saying. There's nothing sophistic about him. He senses where this is going (anticipating his own death, he instructs his sailors to tell Teukros to "care" for him and to take charge of them, 839–840) but he does not know definitively. Consequently he catches himself up in his own bind—somewhat as King Oedipus, in a nonmeditative, more externalized plot-driven way, catches *him*self up. This is the deepest, most compelling dimension of Aias's tragedy: where the personal, the social, the mythic, and the historical implode with the free-fall precision of a controlled demolition. Gravity rules. It's not only Aias who is doomed. The heroic world and its ethos go down with him. Most astounding, and telling, is that in this play Sophocles critiques *and* reverences the heroic ethos even as he shows it passing into historical obsolescence because, in reality, it no longer serves. (For a comparable maneuver in actual life, but with an utterly different outcome, see the exchange between Sophocles and Pisander, as reported by Aristotle, summarized on p. xxiii of "When Life Was Theater.")

844 *a kind of peace* Often translated as 'salvation' or 'deliverance.' However an unambiguous 'salvation' would determine

this to be an outright deception on Aias's part. 'Deliverance' might accommodate the fullness of Aias's meaning, but only if it were clear that the deliverance is *from life*—not deliverance *to* a 'heaven.' 'A kind of peace' leaves open the possibility of a continued existence which is not that of salvation (implying an 'afterlife' as we ourselves understand it) but an afterlife as understood by ancient Greeks and, most fiercely, by Aias, who anticipates having words with Death himself in an underworld where salvation, in the sense of ultimate deliverance, is not even a concept, never mind a hope.

845 Ooo *I've got goose bumps; I'm so* "Describes the prickling or shuddering of the flesh . . . what the chorus feels is akin to sexual excitement" (Garvie, 192). Also, see l. 748. Given Sophocles' longstanding interest in healing and in 'reading' symptoms of physical and mental states of well- or ill-being, he often dwells on the signs of sickness or health—or, in this case, heightened emotion. This preoccupation is especially pronounced in *Philoktetes*.

861 *Ares dissolves his blood-dark threat!* Ares, the god of war, allows for peace when he ceases to destroy. The image is of a cloud-darkened sky breaking up.

865–866 *Aias . . . goes, in good faith* They think he will reaffirm the oath by which he committed himself to go to Troy, making a sacrifice to the gods. They do not anticipate that the sacrifice will be Aias himself.

894 *He wasn't to be let go out* The onus is on Aias's allies. Yet *any* attempt to restrain Aias from doing what he wants to do would be impossible to enforce.

945 *whose life is misery!* Cf. 637ff. Tekmessa: "All I have is you. With nowhere / to turn to. Backed by fate your spear . . ."

1006–1008 *the deathless virgins . . . the dread / ever-overtaking*
*Furies* The Furies, or Erinyes. Goddesses of vengeance, relentless and merciless, who pursue justice not only through
this world but on into the next. They are also called Eumenides, the Kindly Ones, either to mollify them or to acknowl-
edge that by punishing offenses against the foundations of
human society they become benefactors of society.

1015 *Helios, chariot wheels climbing the sky* The sun.

1069ff. *Nooo! We'll never get home!* The Chorus's first concern
is how Aias's death will affect them. The same holds for
everyone who has depended on Aias, including Tekmessa,
when Aias is contemplating suicide, and Teukros, when he
arrives on the scene of Aias's death. It testifies to the extraordinary web of relations and lives—including those of
the Greek army and its commanders—that have depended
on the towering figure of Aias.

1086 *the blood gasping up through his nostrils* Usually the
blood is described as "spurting," i.e., pumped by the heart.
But Aias is dead. His heart is stopped. The phrase must
refer, then, to the postmortem pressure of gases and flu-
ids set loose in the thorax as the body resettles into itself.
"Gasping" also intimates what expiring gases mingled with
blood sound like. A related case has been made, on linguistic
grounds, that the language here "resembles that at Aeschylus, *Eumenides* 248–9, where . . . Orestes, the prey of the
Furies, gasps out his guts" (Garvie, 212).

1190 *the bastard of a captive girl* Teukros's mother was He-
sione, the daughter of King Laomedon of Troy. Telamon
'won' her during the first Trojan war (1473–80).

1205–1206 *With the war belt / Aias gave him, Hektor was gripped* Reference to the customary reciprocity of gifts, including between enemies. In this version of the story, which differs from that in Homer, Hektor was tied to his chariot by Achilles (using the war belt Aias had given Hektor) and dragged to death. Now Aias has met his own death on the sword given him by Hektor.

1226 *Hey you!* This, by Menelaos, is "a colloquial and peremptory use of the nominative of the pronoun" (Garvie, 131). It has been anticipated by Athena's "YOU IN THERE, AIAS!" (111) and echoed later by Agamemnon's "You there!" (1402). Sophocles sometimes admits colloquialisms, "particularly in the speech of servants or messengers. . . . Yet even when [he] gives colloquialism to upper-caste heroes, it is frequently for the purpose of revealing them to be vulgar and undignified, like Menelaos in [*Aias*], or losing their composure through such emotions as anger or excitement" (Csapo, 130).

1259–1262 *But in a city of no respect, just / insolence and willfulness . . . Fear is in order.* Menelaos's prescript for effective governance, and his attitude toward the *dêmos*, is that of an oligarch.

1270–1272 *You've set down right-minded precepts . . . outraging the dead.* Menelaos has said the right thing, but in leaving Aias's corpse unburied he violates his own precepts.

1292–1293 *because of an oath . . . shell of a man.* See *Philoktetes*, 81–82.

1300 *The archer, far from blood dust, thinks he's something* Archery was considered less honorable than front line fighting with a sword or spear—though this attitude had less to do with military effectiveness than with 'class' distinctions. Frequently archers were archers (or slingers) because they couldn't afford hoplite armor. They were social inferiors (Hanson, 149). "The Scythian archers who formed the police force were slaves" (Garvie, 227). Eventually archers and cavalry became more decisive than hoplites, who with their breastplates, shields, and tight formations were too ponderous and inflexible to cope with ambushes or shifts in the direction of battle.

1301 *I'm very good at what I do* Discussed in "When Theater Was Life," pp. xvii–xviii.

1350ff. *Press your hand on him, clutching locks of hair* As suppliants under the protection of Zeus, the boy and his mother will be safe. The dead Aias, "a few moments ago . . . so helpless, is now, even before he is buried, in a position to protect his dependents" even as they protect him (Garvie, 231). It is most telling that Eurysakes, who has been named after his father's shield, effectively *becomes* his father's shield, but in a way that Aias himself could not have envisioned. They form a telling tableau of survival based on interdependence—Eurysakes, Tekmessa, Teukros, and the remains of Aias, in concert with Zeus—as distinguished from the old, now obsolete model whereby the survival of all depended on one towering, heroic individual.

1372–1373 *who taught Greeks / to combine forces* Not an imprecation against war in general, but against what Jebb calls "public war" (179), implicitly contrasting this with tribal or *polis* wars, essentially defensive wars fought largely on home or neighboring grounds. The Trojan War, however, involves an alliance among different Greek entities to fight an expeditionary war under a semiautonomous military command that is neither tribe- nor *polis*-based. This alliance, whereby the Greeks have been taught "how to league in war" (Lloyd-Jones, 143), more nearly resembles the organization of modern international warfare. The Greek "league" as presented in the *Iliad* is relatively primitive and ad hoc, based largely on opportunism, oaths, and standing allegiances to lords. Actual fifth-century alliances were nearer our own, but they were not, as in our own time, bureaucratized and 'legalized.' There is *no* qualitative comparison with present-day NATO—which, with its power to call upon the military forces of numerous, far-flung countries, is the global apotheosis of a composite expeditionary force. Nonetheless a rough comparison does throw light on the *specificity* of the Greek warriors' concerns.

1418 *a clear majority* Given the assumption that the vote was rigged, this may be a reminder that even a hands-on electoral republic (by implication Athens itself) is susceptible to bribery and other manipulation. A *dêmokratia* is no guarantee that power will reside in the hands of the *dêmos* (the common people).

1424 *but those with brains* i.e., Odysseus.

1433 *I can't understand your barbarian babble* "Only one reference to the fact that a character speaks a foreign language exists in the extant plays of Sophocles" (Csapo, 130). "The pretense that Teukros does not speak intelligible Greek brings the speech to its offensive end, and for the audience removes any lingering doubts that Agamemnon's arguments may have been sound" (Garvie, 239). As noted in a review of Eric Gruen's *Rethinking the Other in Antiquity,* the problem with the word 'barbarian' is that it connotes "a mixture of primitivism, aggression and stupidity, whereas the Greek *barbaros* signified only a linguistic deficiency, describing those who produced sounds like *bar-bar-bar* rather than comprehensible Greek speech. . . . Translators struggle with *barbaros*, along with other tonal cues that might reveal Herodotus' attitude to non-Greeks, the Persians in particular" (James Romm, "Among the Barbarians," *London Review of Books*, Vol. 33, No. 24, 15 December 2011, pp. 26–27).

1463–1472 *Where are you looking? at what . . . in the silence of fishes* Pelops came from Phrygia, which is part of Troy. It therefore follows that Agamemnon, who is related to the enemy Trojans, is himself a barbarian. Agamemnon's father, Atreus, on discovering his wife had committed adultery with his brother, Thyestes, invited Thyestes to a banquet at which he fed Thyestes his own sons. The father of Agamemnon's mother (Aerope, from Crete) caught her with a slave lover. He sent her to King Nauplius to be drowned. She was spared, however, and (as we are now reminded) lived to be Agamemnon's mother.

1488 *Or was it your brother's wife?* Helen. Teukros either pretends he doesn't know or care which wife has been the cause of this war, or he insinuates that Agamemnon as well as Menelaos has bedded Helen. Either way, the insult may not be casual. If Helen is truly the cause of this war, she's not a valid nor a sufficient one.

# WORKS CITED AND CONSULTED

Aristotle. *Aristotle's Poetics*. Trans. Leon Golden. Tallahassee: Florida State University Press, 1981.

———. *The Art of Rhetoric*. Trans. John Henry Freese. Loeb Classical Library 193. Cambridge, MA: Harvard University Press, 1967.

Blundell, Mary Whitlock. *Helping Friends and Harming Enemies: A Study in Sophocles and Greek Ethics*. Cambridge: Cambridge University Press, 1989.

Boegehold, Alan L. *When a Gesture Was Expected*. Princeton, NJ: Princeton University Press, 1999.

Carpenter, Thomas H., and Christopher A. Faraone, eds. *Masks of Dionysus*. Ithaca, NY: Cornell University Press, 1993.

Cartledge, Paul. *Ancient Greek Political Thought in Practice*. Cambridge: Cambridge University Press, 2009.

Csapo, Eric. *Actors and Icons of the Ancient Theater*. Malden, MA: Blackwell-Wiley, 2010.

Csapo, Eric, and William J. Slater. *The Context of Ancient Drama*. Ann Arbor: University of Michigan Press, 1994.

Eagleton, Terry. *Sweet Violence: The Idea of the Tragic*. Malden, MA: Blackwell, 2003.

Easterling, P. E., ed. *The Cambridge Companion to Greek Tragedy*. Cambridge: Cambridge University Press, 1997.

Edmunds, Lowell. *Theatrical Space and Historical Place in Sophocles' "Oedipus at Colonus."* Lanham, MD: Rowman & Littlefield, 1996.

Else, Gerald F. *The Origin and Early Form of Greek Tragedy.* New York: Norton, 1965.

Foley, Helene P. *Female Acts in Greek Tragedy.* Princeton, NJ: Princeton University Press, 2001.

Garland, Robert. *The Greek Way of Death.* Ithaca, NY: Cornell University Press, 1985.

———. *The Greek Way of Life.* Ithaca, NY: Cornell University Press, 1990.

Garvie, A. F., ed. and trans. *Ajax.* By Sophocles. Oxford, UK: Aris & Phillips, 1998.

Golder, Herbert, and Richard Pevear, trans. *Aias (Ajax).* By Sophocles. New York: Oxford University Press, 1999.

Goldhill, Simon. *Reading Greek Tragedy.* Cambridge: Cambridge University Press, 1986.

Gould, Thomas. *The Ancient Quarrel Between Poetry and Philosophy.* Princeton, NJ: Princeton University Press, 1990.

Grene, David, trans. *Philoctetes.* The Complete Greek Tragedies. Eds. David Grene and Richmond Lattimore. University of Chicago Press, 1957.

Guthrie, W. K. C. *The Greeks and Their Gods.* Boston: Beacon Press, 1950.

Hall, Edith. *Greek Tragedy: Suffering Under the Sun.* Oxford University Press, 2009.

Hammond, Paul. *The Strangeness of Tragedy.* Oxford University Press, 2009.

Hanson, Victor Davis. *A War Like No Other*. New York: Random House, 2005.

Herodotus. *The Landmark Herodotus: The Histories*. Ed. Robert B. Strassler. New York: Pantheon Books, 2007.

Hesk, Jon. *Sophocles: Ajax*. London: Gerald Duckworth & Co., 2003.

Hughes, Bettany. *The Hemlock Cup: Socrates, Athens and the Search for the Good Life*. New York: Knopf, 2010.

Jebb, R. C., trans. *Antigone*. By Sophocles. Cambridge: Cambridge University Press, 1928. (Originally published 1888.)

————, trans. *Ajax*. By Sophocles. Cambridge: Cambridge University, 1896.

————, trans. *Electra*. By Sophocles. Cambridge: Cambridge University, 1894.

————, trans. *Oedipus Coloneus*. By Sophocles. Cambridge: Cambridge University, 1886.

————, trans. *Philoctetes*. By Sophocles. Cambridge: Cambridge University, 1898.

————, trans. *Oedipus Tyrannus*. By Sophocles. Cambridge: Cambridge University, 1883.

————, trans. *Trachiniae*. By Sophocles. Cambridge: Cambridge University, 1892.

Kagan, Donald. *Pericles of Athens and the Birth of Democracy*. New York: Touchstone–Simon & Schuster, 1991.

Kirkwood, G. M. *A Study of Sophoclean Drama*. Cornell Studies in Classical Philology 31. Ithaca, NY: Cornell University Press, 1994.

Knox, Bernard M. W. *Essays: Ancient and Modern*. Baltimore: Johns Hopkins University Press, 1989.

————. *The Heroic Temper: Studies in Sophoclean Tragedy.* Berkeley: University of California Press, 1964.

Lefkowitz, Mary R. *The Lives of Greek Poets.* Baltimore: Johns Hopkins University Press, 1981.

Lloyd-Jones, Hugh, trans. *Ajax.* By Sophocles. Loeb Classical Library 20. Cambridge, MA: Harvard University Press, 1994.

————, trans. *Philoctetes.* By Sophocles. Loeb Classical Library 21. Cambridge, MA: Harvard University Press, 1994.

Lloyd-Jones, Hugh, and N. G. Wilson. *Sophoclea: Studies on the Text of Sophocles.* Oxford: Clarendon Press, 1990.

Logue, Christopher. *Patrocleia.* London: Villiers, Ltd. Scorpion Press, 1962.

Moore, J. A., trans. *Selections from the Greek Elegiac, Iambic, and Lyric Poets.* Cambridge, MA: Harvard University Press, 1947.

Phillips, Carl, trans. Introduction and notes by Diskin Clay. *Philoctetes.* By Sophocles. New York: Oxford University Press, 2003.

Pickard-Cambridge, Arthur. *The Dramatic Festivals of Athens.* 2nd ed. Revised with a new supplement by John Gould and D. M. Lewis. Oxford: Clarendon Press, 1988.

Plutarch. *The Rise and Fall of Athens: Nine Greek Lives.* Trans. Ian Scott-Kilvert. London: Penguin, 1960.

Radice, Betty. *Who's Who in the Ancient World.* London: Penguin, 1971.

Rehm, Rush. *The Play of Space: Spatial Transformation in Greek Tragedy.* Princeton, NJ: Princeton University Press, 2002.

Reinhardt, Karl. *Sophocles.* New York: Barnes & Noble–Harper & Row, 1979.

Seaford, Richard. *Reciprocity and Ritual: Homer and Tragedy in the Developing City-State.* Oxford: Clarendon Press, 1994.

Segal, Charles. *"Oedipus Tyrannus": Tragic Heroism and the Limits of Knowledge.* 2nd ed. New York: Oxford University Press, 2001.

———. *Sophocles' Tragic World: Divinity, Nature, Society.* Cambridge, MA: Harvard University Press, 1995.

———. *Tragedy and Civilization: An Interpretation of Sophocles.* Cambridge, MA: Harvard University Press, 1981.

Taplin, Oliver. *Greek Tragedy in Action.* Berkeley: University of California Press, 1978.

Thucydides. *The Landmark Thucydides: A Comprehensive Guide to the Peloponnesian War.* Ed. Robert B. Strassler. New York: Touchstone–Simon & Schuster, 1996.

Ussher, R. G., ed. and trans. *Philoctetes.* By Sophocles. Warminster, UK: Aris & Phillips, 1990.

Vernant, Jean-Pierre, ed. *The Greeks.* Trans. Charles Lambert and Teresa Lavender Fagan. Chicago: University of Chicago Press, 1995.

Vernant, Jean-Pierre, and Pierre Vidal-Naquet. *Myth and Tragedy in Ancient Greece.* Trans. Janet Lloyd. New York: Zone Books, 1990.

Webster, T. B. L., ed. *Philoctetes.* By Sophocles. Cambridge: Cambridge University Press, 1970.

Whitman, C. E. *Sophocles.* Cambridge, MA: Harvard University Press, 1951.

Wiles, David. *Greek Theatre Performances: An Introduction.* Cambridge: Cambridge University Press, 2000.

———. *Tragedy in Athens: Performance Space and Theatrical Meaning.* Cambridge: Cambridge University Press, 1997.

Winkler, John J., and Froma I. Zeitlin, eds. *Nothing to Do with Dionysos?: Athenian Drama in Its Social Context*. Princeton, NJ: Princeton University Press, 1990.

Winnington-Ingram, R. P. *Sophocles: An Interpretation*. Cambridge: Cambridge University Press, 1980.

Woodruff, Paul. *The Ajax Dilemma: Justive, Fairness, and Rewards*. Oxford University Press, 2011.

Zimmern, Alfred. *The Greek Commonwealth: Politics and Economics in Fifth-Century Greece*. 5th ed. New York: Modern Library, 1931.

# ACKNOWLEDGMENTS

Fifty years ago Christopher Logue's *Patrocleia* taught me something about the ancient Greeks. But that immensely slender book taught still more about the body English of format and typography—above all the urgency of writing, translating, with one's *whole* being and resources.

Ten years later, co-translating Aeschylus' *Prometheus Bound* with John Herington, I learned a comparable lesson: translation begins with the whole work, from its generative sources to the passionate arc of living matter that is brought into play. This doesn't mean slighting details, or playing fast and loose with words, but feeling through to their particularity: to what the words are doing, as well as to what they're saying.

# ABOUT THE TRANSLATOR

Aided by a National Defense Fellowship, James Scully received his PhD (1964) from the University of Connecticut, where he later taught for many years. He has received a Lamont Poetry Award from the Academy of American Poets (1967) and Guggenheim, Ingram Merrill Foundation, and NEA fellowships, as well as translation awards and a Bookbuilders of Boston award for book cover design. He and the late C. John Herington co-translated Aeschylus' *Prometheus Bound*.

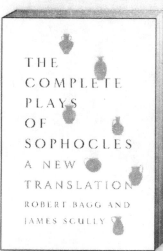
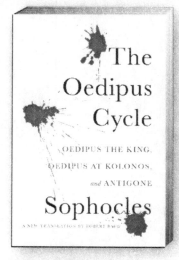

CPSIA information can be obtained at www.ICGtesting.com
Printed in the USA
LVOW06s1130241114

415180LV00014B/16/P